Minnesota Days

OUR HERITAGE IN STORIES, ART, AND PHOTOS

Michael Dregni, Editor

With stories, artwork, and photographs from Garrison Keillor, Jim Brandenburg, F. Scott Fitzgerald, Laura Ingalls Wilder, Sinclair Lewis, Jim Klobuchar, Wanda Gág, Jon Hassler, Gordon Parks, William Albert Allard, Wing Young Huie, Francis Lee Jaques, Jim Northrup, Craig Blacklock, Ole Rölvaag, Winona LaDuke, Sigurd F. Olson, Bill Holm, Paul Gruchow, Bob Artley, Meridel LeSueur, George Morrison, Ernest Whiteman, Josephine Lutz Rollins, Miriam Ibling, Wayne Gudmundson, Frank Big Bear, Carl Gawboy, and more.

Voyageur Press

First published in 1999 by Voyageur Press, an imprint of MBI Publishing Company, Galtier Plaza, Suite 200, 380 Jackson Street, St. Paul, MN 55101-3885 USA

Text and photographs copyright © 1999 by Voyageur Press

Edited by Michael Dregni
Designed by Kristy Tucker
Printed in Hong Kong

Library of Congress Cataloging-in-Publication Data
Minnesota days : our heritage in stories, art, and photos / Michael Dregni, editor.
     p. cm.
    ISBN-13 978-0-89658-421-1
    ISBN-10 0-89658-421-6
    1. Minnesota—History Miscellanea. 2. Minnesota—History
Pictorial Works. I. Dregni, Michael, 1961- .
F606.5.M55 1999
977.6—dc21   99-20679
                CIP

MBI Publishing Company titles are also available at discounts in bulk quantity for industrial or sales-promotional use. For details write to Special Sales Manager at MBI Publishing Company, Galtier Plaza, Suite 200, 380 Jackson Street, St. Paul, MN 55101-3885 USA

On the frontispiece: Dawn breaks over Brule Lake in the Boundary Waters Canoe Area. (Photograph © Gary Alan Nelson)

On the title pages: Sunrise lights the Lake Superior shoreline near Grand Marais. (Photograph © Greg Ryan/Sally Beyer)

Title page inset: "Spring in the Garden," a lithograph by Wanda Gág. (Minnesota Historical Society)

OPPOSITE PAGE: SPLIT ROCK LIGHTHOUSE
A full moon rises above Lake Superior as Split Rock Lighthouse stands guard. The need for a lighthouse at Split Rock was tied to the mining of iron ore on the Range: The increased shipping traffic that was hauling ore east was devastated by the notorious November gales in 1905, prompting the U.S. Lighthouse Service to start construction at Split Rock in 1909 to guide ships safely to Duluth and Two Harbors. The Lighthouse Board also noted that "the unusual magnetic attractions" of the Iron Range's ore skewed ship compass readings. Since roads did not reach the promontory, derricks were built atop the 130-foot-high cliff to lift some three hundred tons of building material from lighters. After it entered service in 1910, Split Rock Lighthouse served Lake Superior for sixty years. The Coast Guard decommissioned it in 1969, and the lighthouse and its living quarters were restored by the Minnesota Historical Society. (Photograph © Gary Alan Nelson)

CONTENTS PAGE: COMMON LOON
The common loon has long been a symbol of the northwoods, haunting the world with its call and inspiring countless legends and stories. (Photograph © Daniel J. Cox/Natural Exposures)

Acknowledgments

I would like to thank all of the people who helped make this book come to life: William Albert Allard and Sarah Hoff, *National Geographic* magazine; Ruth Bauer Anderson, Minnesota Historical Society; Bob Artley, whom I remember from my own days at the Worthington *Daily Globe*; Lee Bjerk at Images of the Past, Stillwater; Craig Blacklock; Todd Bockley; Jeffrey Chapman; Martha Cloutier, Library Associate at North Dakota State University; Eric Dregni, for intimate knowledge of the great Ball of Twine race; Juanita Espinoza of the Native Arts Circle; Carl Gawboy; Ken Giannini, Minnesota State Fair; Wayne Gudmundson; the Dave Hohman Postcard Archives; Bill Holm; Wing Young Huie; Winona LaDuke; Greg Larson, Milkweed Editions; Don Luce, Curator of Exhibits at the James Ford Bell Museum of Natural History, for his assistance and knowledge concerning artist Francis Lee Jaques; Jeff Moen, University of Minnesota Press; Jim Northrup; Ellen B. Olson; Faye Passow; Tim Ready, Science Museum of Minnesota; Ann Regan, Minnesota Historical Society Press; and last but far from least, Ernest Whiteman.

Finally, a thanks to everyone at Voyageur Press.

Contents

Minnesota Days

The stories, photographs, and works of art in *Minnesota Days* were selected in an attempt to offer insights into our common history, to tell a universal story through these personal tales. The individual items collected here are each significant in their own right, but when brought together, they tell a larger story and paint a broader picture. The tales of our ancestors and their Minnesota show us the path that has led to the Minnesota as we know it. They speak of our heritage and our future, of Minnesota days past and to come.

Minnesota is a state rich in literature and art, and the pieces within this book stretch out like strands of a spider's web comprising numerous cultures, peoples, and backgrounds. The essays by Charles A. Eastman and Meridel LeSueur portray the conflict between different peoples and ways of life—themes echoed decades later in the writing of Winona LaDuke and the sculpture of Ernest Whiteman. The selection from Ole Rölvaag's famous novel *Giants in the Earth* offers a portrait of Minnesota as a Promised Land for those who made the immigrant's exodus; even though his characters were Norwegians of the late 1800s, his themes resound across the many cultures and generations that make up Minnesota, and are reflected in the passionate photojournalism of Wing Young Huie.

Only a handful of other states can point to such a legacy of writers. Minnesota has a particularly long tradition of fiction and essays devoted to the land. This lineage stretches from

ABOVE: "Greetings from Minnesota" postcard, 1950s

OPPOSITE PAGE: World's Largest Walleye
Minnesota is famous—or infamous—for its "colossals of the roads," gigantic roadside animals and other icons, often fabricated of fiberglass. Most bear legends promising them to be the "World's Largest," but with our habit for stretching the truth when it comes to fishing tales, there's no way of knowing if the gigantic walleye welcoming visitors to Garrison is truly the world's largest. Still, no other state has such heartfelt fondness for its fiberglass roadside animals as Minnesota. (Photograph © Richard Hamilton Smith)

the early journals of European explorers through the great novels of the settlers, from Laura Ingalls Wilder's "Little House" series to Martha Ostenso's chronicles of the Red River Valley, from the wilderness essays of Sigurd Olson to the modern-day writings of Paul Gruchow. Such a subject may be only natural to Minnesotans, whose life sometimes seems to be a never-ending battle with the elements.

Minnesota also has a long history of writers of satire, a lineage that includes F. Scott Fitzgerald, Sinclair Lewis, Jon Hassler, Garrison Keillor, and Joel and Ethan Coen. Some of these satirists, such as Lewis, write with a barbed pen; others, such as Hassler, poke gentle, gracious fun and appear to include themselves among those they are portraying. Perhaps the root of such satire lies in small-town café gab or frontier newspaper gossip, both of which can boast an abundant history in the state.

In addition, Minnesota has a strong tradition of authors of Native American heritage, from Charles Eastman—who was one of the first well-known Native writers in the United States—to Gerald Vizenor, Louise Erdrich, Jim Northrup, David Treuer, and many others.

The life of the state has been chronicled by many renowned photographers. Several of Minnesota's newspapers have fostered this love of photography, including the Minneapolis *StarTribune*, St. Paul *Pioneer Press*, and Minnesota *Daily*. Above all, however, the *Daily Globe* of Worthington championed photographic essays and helped pioneer the use of color in newspapers, providing a stepping stone to many well-known photographers, including Jim Brandenburg and Annie Griffiths Belt, who both went on to work for *National*

BACK ROADS BINGO!
Minneapolis artist Faye Passow's wry encyclopedia of Minnesota culture is presented on an ideal medium: road-trip bingo cards.

Geographic magazine, where their photographs appeared alongside those of Minnesota native William Albert Allard. The most famous of all Minnesota photographers may be John Runk of Stillwater. In the early twentieth century, Runk ran a classic small-town photo studio, and had a rare eye for capturing the details of everyday life through his lens. His voluminous collection of images focused primarily on his beloved river town but offered a vision of the growing state for everyone.

Minnesota artists are also legion, from the famous beadwork of the Anishinaabe, through the Works Projects Administration paintings of the 1930s, to the proliferation of artists' visions in recent years. The works of artists such as Frank Big Bear and Jeffrey Chapman are haunted by past symbols and themes, while pieces by artists such as Josephine

Lutz Rollins and George Morrison blend American and European sensibilities.

This book bears no conceit of being complete or all inclusive or even a showcase of the best. It is, however, representative. There are no rigid rules set for the stories and art that do appear here; the authors and artists need not necessarily be native-born Minnesotans, for instance. The ultimate goal in this collection of writings, photographs, and works of art is to tell a larger story, a tale of Minnesota, its heritage and its people.

Michael Dregni

CHAPTER ONE

THE ONCE AND FUTURE LAND

"The long grass, veering slowly away from the plowshare, sighed over and fell forever, and the earth came to dark and vivid life, the black top-soil breathing out toward the luminous arch of the sky its naked amazement. Thereupon the setting sun took the ragged, inky scars in the earth and joined them with the image of the oxen, the plow, and the man. All, now, were one."
—Martha Ostenso, *O River, Remember!*, 1943

Minnesota's history has been short when measured in years but long when measured in the comings and goings of its people. The state has been home to a multitude of cultures, all seeking a place on Earth that they could call their own. The clashes between cultures and the battles for identity that have forged the history of Minnesota are reflected in these stories and essays.

LEFT: **NATIVE AMERICAN HUNTER**
Portrait of a Dakota hunter taken at the Whitney Studio, circa 1900. (Minnesota Historical Society)
OPPOSITE PAGE: **DAWN OVER THE MISSISSIPPI RIVER**
The sun rises through the morning mists above the many channels of the Mississippi. The Anishinaabe once called the river Wahpadah Tanka, *or Great River, a fitting name for the mighty waters.* (Photograph © Richard Hamilton Smith)

First Impressions of Civilization

By Charles A. Eastman

Charles Alexander Eastman was the best-known Native American writer of the early twentieth century. His premier book, *Indian Boyhood* (1902), was one of the first true autobiographies of a Native American.

A Wahpeton Dakota, Eastman was born Hakadah, or the "Pitiful Last One," in Redwood Falls in 1858; he was later given the name Ohiyesa, or "The Winner." Following the U.S.–Dakota Conflict of 1862, his father, Many Lightnings, was convicted and believed hung at Mankato. After the family fled to the Canadian wilderness, Ohiyesa was raised by his uncle. He later discovered that his father was still alive and was reunited with him.

Taking his father's new Christian name, Eastman was sent to boarding schools before winning scholarships to university. After completing his B.A. at Dartmouth, he received his M.D. in 1890 from Boston University. Eastman practiced medicine on the Pine Ridge Reservation in South Dakota and in St. Paul before turning his back on the white man's world in 1921 to live out his life in near seclusion in a traditional style. He died in 1939 from complications related to smoke inhalation in his teepee.

Eastman was prolific in his writing and public lecturing, retelling Native legends in his books *Red Hunters and Animal People* (1904), *Old Indian Days* (1907), and *Wigwam Evenings*

"Untitled"

Minnesota-based Northern Arapaho artist Ernest Whiteman's sculptures blend traditional Native American symbols and pictographs with modern materials, creating a unique vision that is at the same time old and new. The arms of this figure depict symbols of rain and harvest, symbolizing a person living in harmony with the world. The ghostly outline is cut from quarter-inch-thick steel while the heart-line is illuminated with gaudy red neon. Some of Whiteman's other sculptures follow similar themes, reinventing rock paintings and carvings to retell ancient legends for the modern world.

(1909). His other books ranged from further autobiographical volumes—such as *From the Deep Woods to Civilization: Chapters in the Autobiography of an Indian* (1916) to sociological commentaries, including *The Soul of the Indian: An Interpretation* (1911) and *The Indian Today: The Past and Future of the Red American* (1915). Many Native Americans regarded Eastman as an apologist working to control and convert them; others saw him as an ambassador attempting to explain Native values so the white world would appreciate and accept their traditional culture. Either way, Eastman led an extraordinary life.

This excerpt from his autobiography tells of Ohiyesa's reunion with his father, who brought him into the world of the white man.

I WAS SCARCELY old enough to know anything definite about the "Big Knives," as we called the white men, when the terrible Minnesota massacre broke up our home and I was carried into exile. I have already told how I was adopted into the family of my father's younger brother, when my father was betrayed and imprisoned. We all supposed that he had shared the fate of those who were executed at Mankato, Minnesota.

Now the savage philosophers looked upon vengeance in the field of battle as a lofty virtue. To avenge the death of a relative or of a dear friend was considered a great deed. My uncle, accordingly, had spared no pains to instill into my young mind the obligation to avenge the death of my father and my older brothers. Already I looked eagerly forward to the day when I should find an opportunity to carry out his teachings. Meanwhile, he himself went upon the war-path and returned with scalps every summer. So it may be imagined how I felt toward the Big Knives!

On the other hand, I had heard marvelous things of this people. In some things we despised them; in others we regarded them as *wakan* (mysterious), a race whose power bordered upon the supernatural. I learned that they had made a "fireboat." I could not understand how they could unite two elements which cannot exist together. I thought the water would put out the fire, and the fire would consume the boat if it had the shadow of a chance. This was to me a preposterous thing! But when I was told that the Big Knives had created a "fire-boat-walks-on-mountains" (a locomotive) it was too much to believe.

"Why," declared my informant, "those who saw this monster move said that it flew from mountain to mountain when it seemed to be excited. They said also that they believed it carried a thunder-bird, for they frequently heard his usual war-whoop as the creature sped along!"

Several warriors had observed from a distance one of the first trains on the Northern Pacific, and had gained an exaggerated impression of the wonders of the pale-face. They had seen it go over a bridge that spanned a deep ravine and it seemed to them that it jumped from one bank to the other. I confess that the story almost quenched my ardor and bravery.

Two or three young men were talking together about this fearful invention.

"However," said one, "I understand that this fire-boat-walks-on mountains cannot move except on the track made for it."

Although a boy is not expected to join in the conversation of his elders, I ventured to ask: "Then it cannot chase us into any rough country?"

"No, it cannot do that," was the reply, which I heard with a great deal of relief.

I had seen guns and various other things brought to us by the French Canadians, so that I had already some notion of the supernatural gifts of the white man; but I had never before heard such tales as I listened to that morning. It was said that they had bridged the Missouri and Mississippi rivers, and that they made immense houses of stone and brick, piled on top of one another until they were as high as high hills. My brain was puzzled with these things for many a day. Finally I asked my uncle why the Great Mystery gave such power to the *Washichu* (the rich)—sometimes we called them by this name—and not to us Dakotas.

"For the same reason," he answered, "that he gave to Duta the skill to make fine bows and arrows, and to Wachesne no skill to make anything."

"And why do the Big Knives increase so much more in number than the Dakotas?" I continued.

"It has been said, and I think it must be true, that they have larger families than we do. I went into the house of an *Eashicha* (a German), and I counted no less than nine children. The eldest of them could not have been over fifteen. When my grandfather first visited them, down at the mouth of the Mississippi, they were comparatively few; later my father visited their Great Father at Washington, and they had already spread over the whole country.

"Certainly they are a heartless nation. They have made some of their people servants—yes, slaves! We have never believed in keeping slaves, but it seems that these *Washichu* do! It is our belief that they painted their servants black a long time ago, to tell them from the rest, and now the slaves have children born to them of the same color!

"The greatest object of their lives seems to be to acquire possessions—to be rich. They desire to possess the whole

HEADWATERS
The humble source of the great Mississippi River at Lake Itasca in Clearwater County. (Photograph © John Gregor/ColdSnap Photography)

ABOVE: WINNEWISSA FALLS

The quarries at Pipestone National Monument have been prized for their special Catlinite "pipestone" that was used by Native Americans from throughout the Great Plains for carvings and calumet pipe bowls. In 1836, explorer and artist George Catlin, for whom the pipestone was later named, recorded a Dakota account of the origin of the stone: "At an ancient time the Great Spirit, in the form of a large bird, stood upon the wall of rock and called all the tribes around him, and breaking out a piece of the red stone formed it into a pipe and smoked it, the smoke rolling over the whole multitude. He then told his red children that this red stone was their flesh, that they were made from it, that they must all smoke to him through it, that they must use it for nothing but pipes: and as it belonged alike to all the tribes, the ground was sacred, and no weapons must be used or brought upon it." (Photograph © Richard Hamilton Smith)

OPPOSITE PAGE: PIPESTONE QUARRY

Sisseton Wahpeton sculptor Mark Pederson uses a sledgehammer and wedge to cut away overburden rock to get to a thin vein of Catlinite at Pipestone National Monument. Pederson has a special permit to quarry the pipestone, which he uses to carve calumet pipe bowls. The Catlinite may range in color from rosy pink to deep sienna. (Photograph © Richard Hamilton Smith)

world. For thirty years they were trying to entice us to sell them our land. Finally the outbreak gave them all, and we have been driven away from our beautiful country.

"They are a wonderful people. They have divided the day into hours, like the moons of the year. In fact, they measure everything. Not one of them would let so much as a turnip go from his field unless he received full value for it. I understand that their great men make a feast and invite many, but when the feast is over the guests are required to pay for what they have eaten before leaving the house. I myself saw at White Cliff (the name given to St. Paul, Minnesota) a man who kept a brass drum and a bell to call people to his table; but when he got them in he would make them pay for the food!

"I am also informed," said my uncle, "but this I hardly believe, that their Great Chief (President) compels every man to pay him for the land he lives upon and all his personal goods—even for his own existence—every year!" (This was his idea of taxation.) "I am sure we could not live under such a law.

"When the outbreak occurred, we thought that our opportunity had come, for we had learned that the Big Knives were fighting among themselves, on account of a dispute over their slaves. It was said that the Great Chief had allowed slaves in one part of the country and not in another, so there was jealousy, and they had to fight it out. We don't know how true this was.

"There were some praying-men who came to us some time before the trouble arose. They observed every seventh day as a holy day. On that day they met in a house that they had built for that purpose, to sing, pray, and speak of their Great Mystery. I was never in one of these meetings. I understand that they had a large book from which they read. By all accounts they were very different from all other white men we have known, for these never observed any such day, and we never knew them to pray, neither did they ever tell us of their Great Mystery.

"In war they have leaders and war-chiefs of different grades. The common warriors are driven forward like a herd of antelopes to face the foe. It is on account of this manner of fighting—from compulsion and not from personal bravery—that we count no coup on them. A lone warrior can do much harm to a large army of them in a bad country."

It was this talk with my uncle that gave me my first clear idea of the white man.

I was almost fifteen years old when my uncle presented me with a flint-lock gun. The possession of the "mysterious iron," and the explosive dirt, or "pulverized coal," as it is called, filled me with new thoughts. All the war-songs that I had ever heard from childhood came back to me with their

heroes. It seemed as if I were an entirely new being—the boy had become a man!

"I am now old enough," said I to myself, "and I must beg my uncle to take me with him on his next war-path. I shall soon be able to go among the whites whenever I wish, and to avenge the blood of my father and my brothers."

I had already begun to invoke the blessing of the Great Mystery. Scarcely a day passed that I did not offer up some of my game, so that he might not be displeased with me. My people saw very little of me during the day, for in solitude I found the strength I needed. I groped about in the wilderness, and determined to assume my position as a man. My boyish ways were departing, and a sullen dignity and composure was taking their place.

The thought of love did not hinder my ambitions. I had a vague dream of some day courting a pretty maiden, after I had made my reputation, and won the eagle feathers.

One day, when I was away on the daily hunt, two strangers from the United States visited our camp. They had boldly ventured across the northern border. They were Indians, but clad in the white man's garments. It was as well that I was

absent with my gun.

My father, accompanied by an Indian guide, after many days' searching had found us at last. He had been imprisoned at Davenport, Iowa, with those who took part in the massacre or in the battles following, and he was taught in prison and converted by the pioneer missionaries, Drs. Williamson and Riggs. He was under sentence of death, but was among the number against whom no direct evidence was found, and who were finally pardoned by President Lincoln.

When he was released, and returned to the new reservation upon the Missouri river, he soon became convinced that life on a government reservation meant physical and moral degradation. Therefore he determined, with several others, to try the white man's way of gaining a livelihood. They accordingly left the agency against the persuasions of the agent, renounced all government assistance, and took land under the United States Homestead law, on the Big Sioux river. After he had made his home there, he desired to seek his lost child. It was then a dangerous undertaking to cross the line, but his Christian love prompted him to do it. He secured a good guide, and found his way in time through the vast wilderness.

As for me, I little dreamed of anything unusual to happen on my return. As I approached our camp with my game on my shoulder, I had not the slightest premonition that I was suddenly to be hurled from my savage life into a life unknown to me hitherto.

When I appeared in sight my father, who had patiently listened to my uncle's long account of my early life and training, became very much excited. He was eager to embrace the child who, as he had just been informed, made it already the object of his life to avenge his father's blood. The loving father could not remain in the teepee and watch the boy coming, so he started to meet him. My uncle arose to go with his brother to insure his safety.

My face burned with the unusual excitement caused by the sight of a man wearing the Big Knives' clothing and coming toward me with my uncle.

"What does this mean, uncle?"

"My boy, this is your father, my brother, whom we mourned as dead. He has come for you."

My father added: "I am glad that my son is strong and brave. Your brothers have adopted the white man's way; I came for you to learn this new way, too; and I want you to grow up a good man."

He had brought me some civilized clothing. At first, I disliked very much to wear garments made by the people I had hated so bitterly. But the thought that, after all, they had not killed my father and brothers, reconciled me, and I put on the clothes.

In a few days we started for the States. I felt as if I were dead and traveling to the Spirit Land; for now all my old ideas were to give place to new ones, and my life was to be entirely different from that of the past.

Still, I was eager to see some of the wonderful inventions of the white people. When we reached Fort Totten, I gazed about me with lively interest and a quick imagination.

My father had forgotten to tell me that the fire-boat-walks-on-mountains had its track at Jamestown, and might appear at any moment. As I was watering the ponies, a peculiar shrilling noise pealed forth from just beyond the hills. The ponies threw back their heads and listened; then they ran snorting over the prairie. Meanwhile, I too had taken alarm. I leaped on the back of one of the ponies, and dashed off at full speed. It was a clear day; I could not imagine what had caused such an unearthly noise. It seemed as if the world were about to burst in two!

I got upon a hill as the train appeared. "O!" I said to myself, "that is the fire-boat-walks-on-mountains that I have heard about!" Then I drove back the ponies.

My father was accustomed every morning to read from his Bible, and sing a stanza of a hymn. I was about very early with my gun for several mornings; but at last he stopped me as I was preparing to go out, and bade me wait.

I listened with much astonishment. The hymn contained the word *Jesus.* I did not comprehend what this meant; and my father then told me that Jesus was the Son of God who came on earth to save sinners, and that it was because of him that he had sought me. This conversation made a deep impression upon my mind.

Late in the fall we reached the citizen settlement at Flandreau, South Dakota, where my father and some others dwelt among the whites. Here my wild life came to an end, and my school days began.

> *"Your brothers have adopted the white man's way; I came for you to learn this new way, too; and I want you to grow up a good man."*

ANISHINAABE FAMILY
An Anishinaabe/Ojibwe family stands before their birchbark lodge on the Leech Lake Reservation during the first half of the twentieth century.
(Special Collections/Minneapolis Public Library)

The Ancient People and the Newly Come

By Meridel LeSueur

Meridel LeSueur wrote of her Midwestern roots in a voice mixing Native American philosophy, radical politics, and her own joyous sense of life.

LeSueur was born in 1900 in Murray, Iowa. She spent her early years in Texas, Oklahoma, and Kansas, before moving to Minnesota at age fifteen. During her lifelong travels, she returned many times to the state as to a refuge.

Over her long life, LeSueur lived in an anarchist commune with feminist Emma Goldman; risked life and limb as a daredevil Hollywood stunt woman in *The Perils of Pauline*; waited tables; acted in the theater; reported for Leftist journals; organized labor with socialists and the radical Industrial Workers of the World union; and was blacklisted in the heyday of McCarthyism.

Above all, LeSueur strived to be a writer. Her first short story was published in 1927, but for decades after she had a difficult time finding a market for her revolutionary feminist subjects. Her masterpiece novel, *The Girl*, was a harshly realistic novel of life during the Depression—one woman's story of the radical labor movement, prostitution, incarceration, and struggle for self-survival; it was written in the 1930s but not published until 1978.

In recent years, many of LeSueur's early writings have been finally published for the first time or resurrected in collections. Among her works are her impressionistic histories of the

---

THUNDERBIRD

Appearing like islands amid the prairie grasses near Jeffers, bare rock protrudes from the earth. These rock faces were used by Native Americans to record stories and symbols of their time for posterity. The petroglyphs depict shamans, thunderbirds, deer, elk, buffalo, turtles, atl-atls, and arrows, relating history that spans some five thousand years. Native Americans carved the petroglyphs by striking chisels of stone or antler with hammerstones, and are believed to have made them between 3000 B.C. and A.D. 1750. (Photograph © Richard Hamilton Smith)

Midwest and its folklore, *Salute to Spring* (1940), *North Star Country* (1945), *Corn Village* (1970), *Song for My Time* (1977), *Women on the Breadlines* (1984), *The Dread Road* (1991), and a variety of children's books, many written pseudonymously while she was blacklisted.

This excerpt from her 1970s autobiographical essay "The Ancient People and the Newly Come" was collected in *Ripening: Selected Work* (1990). Her writing here is at once impressionistic and realistic, like a painting by Grant Wood or Thomas Hart Benton. The prose overflows with emotions that cannot be contained, ranging from angelic happiness to deep anger, summarizing her personal vision of Midwestern history.

BORN OUT OF the caul of winter in the north, in the swing and circle of the horizon, I am rocked in the ancient land. As a child I first read the scriptures written on the scroll of frozen moisture by wolf and rabbit, by the ancient people and the newly come. In the beginning of the century the Indian smoke still mingled with ours. The frontier of the whites was violent, already injured by vast seizures and massacres. The winter nightmares of fear poisoned the plains nights with psychic airs of theft and utopia. The stolen wheat in the cathedrallike granaries cried out for vengeance.

Most of all one was born into space, into the great resonance of space, a magnetic midwestern valley through which the winds clashed in lassoes of thunder and lightning at the apex of the sky, the very wrath of God.

The body repeats the landscape. They are the source of each other and create each other. We were marked by the seasonal body of earth, by the terrible migrations of people, by the swift turn of a century, verging on change never before experienced on this greening planet. I sensed the mound and swell above the mother breast, and from embryonic eye took sustenance and benediction, and went from mother enclosure to prairie spheres curving into each other.

I was born in winter, the village snow darkened toward midnight, footsteps on boardwalks, the sound of horses pulling sleighs, and the ring of bells. The square wooden saltbox house held the tall shadows, thrown from kerosene lamps, of my grandmother and my aunt and uncle (missionaries home from India) inquiring at the door.

It was in the old old night of the North Country. The time of wood before metal. Contracted in cold, I lay in the prairie curves of my mother, in the planetary belly, and outside the vast horizon of the plains, swinging dark and thicketed, circle within circle. The round moon sinister reversed upside down in the sign of Neptune, and the twin fishes of Pisces swimming toward Aquarius in the dark.

But the house was New England square, four rooms upstairs and four rooms downstairs, exactly set upon a firm puritan foundation, surveyed on a level, set angles of the old geometry, and thrust up on the plains like an insult, a declamation of the conqueror, a fortress of our God, a shield against excess and sin.

I had been conceived in the riotous summer and fattened on light and stars that fell on my underground roots, and every herb, corn plant, cricket, beaver, red fox leaped in me in the old Indian dark. I saw everything was moving and entering. The rocking of mother and prairie breast curved around me within the square. The field crows flew in my flesh and cawed in my dream.

Crouching together on Indian land in the long winters, we grew in sight and understanding, heard the rumbling of glacial moraines, clung to the edge of holocaust forest fires, below-zero weather, grasshopper plagues, sin, wars, crop failures, drouth, and the mortgage. The severity of the seasons and the strangeness of a new land, with those whose land had been seized looking in our windows, created a tension of guilt and a tightening of sin. We were often snowed in, the villages invisible and inaccessible in cliffs of snow. People froze following the rope to their barns to feed the cattle. But the cyclic renewal and strength of the old prairie earth, held sacred by thousands of years of Indian ritual, the guerrilla soil of the Americas, taught and nourished us.

We flowed through and into the land, often evicted, drouthed out, pushed west. Some were beckoned to regions of gold, space like a mirage throwing up pictures of utopias, wealth, and villages of brotherhood. Thousands passed through the villages, leaving their dead, deposits of sorrow and calcium, leaching the soil, creating and marking with their faces new wheat and corn, producing idiots, mystics, prophets, and inventors. Or, as an old farmer said, we couldn't move; nailed to the barn door by the wind, we have to make a windmill, figure out how to plow without a horse, and invent barbed wire. A Dakota priest said to me, "It will be from here that the prophets come."

Nowhere in the world can spring burst out of the iron bough as in the Northwest. When the plains, rising to the Rockies, swell with heat, and the delicate glow and silence of the melting moisture fills the pure space with delicate winds and the promise of flowers. We all came, like the crocus, out of the winter dark, out of the captive village where along the river one winter the whole population of children died of diphtheria. In the new sun we counted the dead, and at the spring

THRESHING DAY

Threshing day in the 1890s brought the whole neighborhood together to help each other with chores that would have been insurmountable for one farm family alone. With the arrival of the self-powered combine in the 1930s, this sharing of work became a thing of the past. This crew threshed the harvest on a Blue Earth farm. (Fred Hultstrand History in Pictures Collection, NDIRS-NDSU, Fargo)

dance the living danced up a storm and drank and ate heartily for the pain of it. They danced their alien feet into the American earth and rolled in the haymow to beget against the wilderness new pioneers.

All opened in the spring. The prairies, like a great fan, opened. The people warmed, came together in quilting bees, Ladies' Aid meetings, house railings. The plowing and the planting began as soon as the thaw let the farmers into the fields. Neighbors helped each other. As soon as the seed was in, the churches had picnics and baptizings. The ladies donned their calico dresses and spread a great board of food, while the children ran potato races and one-legged races and the men played horseshoes and baseball. Children were born at home with the neighbor woman. Sometimes the doctor got there. When I was twelve, I helped the midwife deliver a baby. I held onto the screaming mother, her lips bitten nearly off, while she delivered in pieces a dead, strangled corpse. Some people who made it through the winter died in the spring, and we all gathered as survivors to sing "The Old Rugged Cross," "Shall We Gather at the River?" and "God Be with You Till We Meet Again."

The Poles and the Irish had the best parties, lasting for two or three days sometimes. But even the Baptist revival meetings were full of singing (dancing prohibited), and hundreds were forgiven, talking in tongues. Once I saw them break the ice to baptize a screaming woman into the water of life for her salvation.

On Saturday nights everybody would shoot the works, except the prohibitionists and the "good" people, mostly Protestant teetotalers who would appear at church on Sunday morning. The frontier gamblers, rascals, and speculators filled the taverns—drink, women, and gambling consuming the wealth of the people and the land. There were gaming palaces for the rich, even horse racing in Stillwater. In St. Paul Nina Clifford, a powerful figure, had two whorehouses, one for gentlemen from "the Hill" and the other for lumberjacks coming in from the woods to spend their hard-earned bucks. It was said that three powers had divided St. Paul among them—Bishop Ireland took "the Hill," Jim Hill took the city for his trains, and Nina Clifford took all that was below "the Hill."

When the corn was "knee-high by the Fourth of July," and the rainfall was

LUMBER

Minnesota was famed for the astounding richness of lumber that came from its old-growth forests in the late 1800s and early 1900s. Illustrating the quality and size of the lumber, Frank Stenlund, an employee of the David Tozer Company's sawmill at South Stillwater, stands alongside two record-breaking boards in 1912, showing why Minnesota's white pines were nationally renowned. These boards measure three feet wide and two and a half inches thick. (Photograph by John Runk/Minnesota Historical Society)

good and the sun just right, there was rejoicing in the great Fourth of July picnics that specialized in oratory. Without loudspeakers there were speeches that could be heard the length of the grove, delivered by orators who practiced their wind. When farm prices fell because of the speculation of the Grain Exchange in Minneapolis, the threatened farmers met on the prairie and in the park, the town plaza and the courthouse to speak out against the power of monopoly. They came for miles, before and after the harvest, in farm wagons with the whole family. They passed out manifestos and spoke of organizing the people to protect themselves from the predators.

There is no place in the world with summer's end, fall harvest, and Indian summer as in Minnesota. They used to have husking bees. The wagons went down the corn rows, and the men with metal knives on their fingers cut the ears off the stalks and tossed them into the wagons Then they husked the ears, dancing afterward, and if a man got a red ear he could kiss his girl. In August there were great fairs, and the farmers came in to show their crops and beasts, and the workers showed their new reapers and mowers.

There was the excitement of the fall, the terror of the winter coming on. In the winter we didn't have what we did not can, preserve, ferment, or bury in sand. We had to hurry to cut the wood and to get the tomatoes, beans, and piccalilli canned before frost in the garden. It was like preparing for a battle. My grandmother wrapped the apples in newspaper and put them cheek by jowl in the barrels. Cabbage was shredded and barreled for sauerkraut. Even the old hens were killed. I was always surprised to see my gentle grandmother put her foot on the neck of her favorite hen and behead her with a single stroke of a long-handled ax.

The days slowly getting shorter, the herbs hung drying as the woods turned golden. Everything changes on the prairies at the end of summer, all coming to ripeness, and the thunderheads charging in the magnetic moisture of the vast skies. The autumnal dances are the best medicine against the threat of winter, isolation again, dangers. The barns were turned into dance halls before the winter hay was cut. The women raised their long skirts and danced toward hell in schottisches, round dances, and square dances. The rafters rang with the music of the old fiddlers and the harmonica players.

When the golden leaves stacked Persian carpets on the ground and the cornfields were bare, we saw again the great hunched land naked, sometimes fall plowed or planted in winter wheat. Slowly the curve seemed to rise out of the glut of summer, and the earth document was visible script, readable in the human tenderness of risk and ruin.

The owl rides the meadow at his hunting hour. The fox clears out the pheasants and the partridges in the cornfield. Jupiter rests above Antares, and the fall moon hooks itself into the prairie sod. A dark wind flows down from Mandan as the Indians slowly move out of the summer campground to go back to the reservation. Aries, buck of the sky, leaps to the outer rim and mates with earth. Root and seed turn into flesh. We turn back to each other in the dark together, in the short days, in the dangerous cold, on the rim of a perpetual wilderness.

I hung, green girl in the prairie light, in the weathers of three fertile and giant prairie women who strode across my horizon in fierce attitudes of planting, reaping, child-bearing, and tender care of the seed.

It is hard to believe that when I was twelve it was that many years into the century, fourteen years from the Spanish-American War, twenty-two years from the Ghost Dance and the Battle of Wounded Knee, and four years until World War I would change the agrarian world.

I hung, green girl in the prairie light, in the weathers of three fertile and giant prairie women who strode across my horizon in fierce attitudes of planting, reaping, childbearing, and tender care of the seed. As a pear ripens in the chemical presence of other pears, I throve on their just and benevolent love, which assured a multiplication of flesh out of time's decay. I knew the first eden light among their flowers and prairie breasts, buttocks, and meadows, in their magnetic warmth and praise.

One was my grandmother from Illinois, whose mother was a full-blooded Iroquois who had married her teacher, an abolitionist preacher. She had come with him to the West and vowed she would die on the day of his death. She did. My grandmother herself was a puritan, fortressed within her long skirts and bathing under a shift. She divorced her husband, an unusual act in her society. He was drinking up the farms her father left her. Afterward she rode over the Midwest in a horse-drawn buggy, a shotgun beside her, for the Woman's Christian Temperance Union, crying in the wilderness for sobriety. We rode in hayracks in temperance parades, dressed in white and shouting slogans—"Tremble, King Alcohol: We shall grow up, and lips that touch liquor shall never touch mine!"

Her daughter, my mother, went to college, with my grand-

"Fall Plowing"

Grant Wood was the quintessential artist of the farmlands. Born and raised in Iowa, he first studied painting during his two years at the Minneapolis School of Design and Handicraft. He made a pilgrimage to Europe, where he soon realized that "All the good ideas I ever had came to me while I was milking a cow," as he wrote in his autobiography, and returned to paint images of the Midwest. With a technique of full, rounded dimensions and heavy shading, his trees, haystacks, and plants appeared ripe and bountiful while his depiction of the rolling hills gave the fields all of the glory of the open sea. This painting of a plow at rest before a farm vista was created in 1931. (Deere & Company)

mother cooking for fraternities to earn the money to send her through, and married a Lothario preacher at nineteen. She had four children; one died very young. She had read the works of Ellen Key and had heard Emma Goldman, and by the time her last child was born, she believed that a woman had the right of her own life and body. She took a course in comparative religion and broke away from the Christian church. Because the laws of Texas made women and children chattels with no property or civil rights, my mother kidnapped us in the night and fled north like a black slave woman, hoping to get over the border into the new state of Oklahoma, where the laws were more liberal. My father tried to extradite us as criminals or property but failed.

The third woman was a Mandan Indian we called Zona. She lived in the grove with the Indians who came in the summer to work in the fields, and she helped us out at canning time. Her husband had died of grief because the buffalo did not come back in the Ghost Dance and because, after the massacre at Wounded Knee, the government had prohibited her people from dancing and smoking the sacred pipe and had suppressed the shield societies. After that, she said, even the blueberries disappeared.

I grew in the midst of this maternal forest, a green sapling, in bad years putting my roots deep down for sustenance and survival. It was strange and wonderful what these women had in common. They knew the swift linear movement of a changing society that was hard on women. They had suffered from men, from an abrasive society, from the wandering and disappearance of the family. They lived a subjective and parallel life, in long loneliness of the children, in a manless night among enemies.

They were not waiting for land to open up, for gold mines to be discovered, or for railroads to span the north. They were not waiting for any kind of progress or conquest. They were waiting for the Apocalypse, for the coming of some messiah, or, like my grandmother, to join their people in heaven after a frugal and pure life. Their experience of this world centered around the male as beast, his drunkenness and chicanery, his oppressive violence.

They carried in them the faces of old seeds, ghosts of immigrants over land bridges, old prayers in prairie ash, nourishing rain, prophecies of embryos and corpses, distance opening to show the burning green madonnas in the cob, doomed radiance of skeletons, concentrated calcium, delayed cries at night, feeding pollen and fire. They carried herbs and seeds in sunbonnets, bags of meal, and lilac pouches.

We sat together after harvest, canning, milking and during cyclones in the cellar, and they seemed like continents, full of appearing children and dying heroines. The three of them had much to do with the primal events of the country-side—death, birth, illness, betterment of roads and schools.

I sneaked out with Zona often, crawling out the window over the summer kitchen and shinnying down the apple tree to go through the pale spring night to the Indian fires, where the Indian workers drummed until the village seemed to sink away and something fierce was thrust up on the old land. The earth became a circle around the central fire, and the skin stretched over the quiet and hollow skulls of the old and sacred traditional people of the Mandans. The horizon grew larger, the sling of the night stars moved above, and the horizon dilated in the repeating circle of the dancers.

I sat hidden in the meadow with Zona. She was tall and strong, like many of the Plains Indians. The structure of her face was Oriental, her woman's cheeks round as fruits, encased nutlike by her long black hair. She told me of how the grass once moved in the wind, winey in color—the ancient flesh of the mother before the terrible steel plow put its ravenous teeth in her. How antelope, deer, elk, and wild fowl lived richly upon the plains, and how in spring the plains seethed with the roaring of mating buffalo. How you could hear the clicking of their horns and the drumbeat of their feet in the fury of rut. How the warriors went out to slay the meat for the winter. And the summers of the wild berries and the plums and the making of pemmican, the jollity and wooing, the buffalo going south to the salt licks and the Mandans to their great mounded grass cathedrals where they spent the winter in telling stories and legends of the mountains and the shining sea to the west. She said they were the first people in the world. They had lived inside the mother earth and had come up on huge vines into the light. The vine had broken and there were some of her people still under the earth. And she told how the traders threw smallpox-infected clothing into the Mandan village. Most of them died that winter. The whole northern plains stank with the unburied dead.

She showed me that the earth was truly round, sacred, she said, so that no one could own it. The land is not for taking, she said, and I am not for taking. You can't have anything good in the square or in five. All must be four or seven. You can't divide the land in the square, she said. She made the whole landscape shift and encircle me. She said the earth went far down and the whites could only buy and deed the top. The earth waited, its fingers clasped together like culms: she closed her brown fingers to show the interlocking. She said that men and women were rooted, interpenetrating, turning to the center. She did not believe in hell or heaven. She believed we were here now in this place. She said the earth would give back a terrible holocaust to the white people for being assaulted, plowed up, and polluted. She said everything returned, everything was now, in this time. She said past, present, and future were invented by the white man.

But it was the grass, she said: Grass was one of the richest foods on earth and the prairie grass had salts and protein more than any other food. Before the plow, the plains grass could have fed nations of cattle—all the cattle in the world—just as it had fed the buffalo. They did not overgraze when there were no fences because they walked away as they ate. She said that now the earthflesh was wrong side up and blowing away in the wind. The grass might never come back, the buffalo never return.

She said the government could not stop the Indians from prayer and the dances. They would take them underground with the unborn people. She swept her sacred feather around the horizon, to show the open fan of the wilderness and how it all returned: mortgaged land, broken treaties—all opened among the gleaming feathers like a warm-breasted bird turning into the turning light of moon and sun, with the grandmother earth turning and turning. What turns, she said, returns. When she said this, I could believe it.

I knew the turning earth and woman would defend me. I saw the powerful strong women, and I was a small green girl with no breasts and hardly a bowel for anger, but gleaming among them, unused, naked as the land, learning anger, and turning to cauterize and protect the earth, to engender out of their rape and suffering a new race to teach the warriors not to tread the earth and women down. At their own peril!

I saw them, the circle like the prairie holding the children within the power of the grandmothers, receiving the returning warriors from all thievery, defeats, and wounds. The fierce and guerrilla strength of the puritan and Indian women seemed similar, unweighed, even unknown, the totemic power of birth and place, earth and flesh.

Their fierce embraces seemed to crush and terrorize my brothers and me. There was something of anguish in them. They had the bodies of the fiercest exiled heroines in fiction and history, pursued, enslaved. They listened to each other and the horrors of their tales—how the Iroquois fled the assassins of my grandmother's village, how she came down the Ohio and brought a melodeon. My mother told of her flight from Texas, across the border into Oklahoma, where women were given the rights to their children. The Indian woman Zona told how her mother was killed in 1890 at the Battle of Wounded Knee, running with her suckling child till the soldiers gunned her down and left the child to freeze at the breast. How her father waited for the Ghost Dance buffalo

to come out of the rock and they never came. The three women sat bolt upright in the afternoon with high and noble faces and told these stories so much alike in a strange way. I put it down in my heart that they were so fierce and angry and tempestuous, so strong, because they were bound for the protection of all and had a fierce and terrible and awful passion for vindication and the payment of ransom and the mysterious rescue of something. . . .

The great richness of growing up in a northwest village was in the variety and the excitement of all the ethnic cultures. I was free to go into all of them, even singing in Norwegian choirs and dancing with Finnish dance groups. The rituals were still celebrated. There was even a bagpipe group that marched on St. Patrick's Day, all in green, and in the park I listened to a lawyer, three sheets in the wind, recite the last speech of Robert Emmet. I liked to sample the rich foods, too, and secretly found in myself a riotous temperament different from my grandmother's.

I especially loved the dances. They were so colorful and varied, and some were so sensual and beautiful. They freed me from severe puritan sexual rigidity, from relating pleasure to guilt and sin. I remember my first dance. I don't know how my mother and my grandmother let me go, but it was not without warnings, threats, and a terrible armor against sin and excess. My first party dress was white, although I would have preferred red or even yellow. But only the Polish whores wore those colors, my grandmother said. So I wore a white dress and shoes that had a thin stripe of red around them and little heels. I had rolled my hair on newspaper to have curls, which seemed to me the height of voluptuousness.

Jon came to pick me up in a surrey with a fringe on top, though it was harnessed to a plow horse. The harvest was just over, and his huge forearms were browned from the sun and gleaming. He smelled of chaff, even though he was scrubbed to within an inch of his life and his wild straw hair was slicked down with bear grease. He seemed strange and huge as he helped me onto the high step. We drove slowly through the aspens, which were gold around us. I smelled of talcum powder and so did he. I had rubbed wet crepe paper on my cheeks and blackened my eyes with kitchen matches, passing my grandmother quickly so she couldn't see my whorish color.

> *I remember my first dance. I don't know how my mother and my grandmother let me go, but it was not without warnings, threats, and a terrible armor against sin and excess.*

THRESHING CREW OF A BYGONE ERA
The McGuire Brothers outfit takes a break alongside their trusty steam traction engine while threshing the autumn harvest near Stillwater in 1931. (Photograph by John Runk/Minnesota Historical Society)

The old horse turned, laughing, to see if we were there, we were so silent. In the grove wagons and carriages had stopped for spooning as it was early. I was glad we weren't going to do that. My grandmother had told me to drink nothing, just as Demeter told Persephone not to eat anything in Hades, though of course she did and was trapped by pomegranate seeds. She warned me that even grape punch could easily be tampered with. She meant spiked.

In the big empty hall everyone stood around kidding and waiting. The men seemed very tall and hung their heads. The girls seemed unbearably bright, each in her best bib and tucker, all laughing too loud and embracing each other to show how good it was to embrace.

But soon the bung was pulled from the beer barrel. Mugs were filled, and moonshine was nipped outside the door. But lips that touch liquor shall never touch mine. Besides, I was bold and spiced enough, going out with a boy, wearing almost high heels, and waiting to dance for the first time.

The fiddlers started warming up. An accordion joined them and we were off. I began to be tossed from one tall man to another. My feet hardly touched the ground, and the caller could have been speaking another language. I didn't need to know the dance, I just followed. I went from one great harvester to the other. They were laughing, some yelling and "feeling you up," as the girls said. Through the hours we were flying, sweating, pressed, tossed, stamping out the rhythms whirling from embrace to embrace, touching—Hitch 'em up and hike 'em up a high tuckahaw, give me the dance of turkey in the straw. Sugar in the gourd, honey in the horn, I never was so happy since the day I was born.

As the night got deeper and the fiddlers hotter, we were flung into the men's arms, back and forth, a weave of human bodies. I couldn't tell one from the other. A girl took me outside with her. The girls lifted their skirts on one side of the field, and the boys stood with their backs to us on the other. I never heard such laughter or sensed such dangerous meaning in the night, in what took place in the woods, when the dancers returned with curious smiles and leaves in their hair. We seemed on the edge of some abysmal fire. But they seemed unafraid plunging into the heat and the danger as if into a bonfire of roses.

I never was the same again.

My grandmother homesteaded a piece of land and built a house on it which was a simple pure expression of the Protestant needs of her severe religion, her graceless intensity of the good, thrifty, work-for-the-night-is-coming, dutiful labor. She came alone to the wilderness, hired stonemasons and carpenters, and demanded a design to match her dimensions and spirit. Did she make a drawing on a piece of paper, or did she spin it out of her memory, prudence, and frugality? It was a New England farmhouse with a summer kitchen, a birthing room on ground level, and a closed front parlor where one did not let the sun come. She probably did not consider that the house was squared off on an ancient land of mounds and pyramids and cones, on land that had not been plowed in a million years. Neither did she think the land had been monstrously taken from its native people. If she thought of it at all, she undoubtedly felt the Christian purposes of her Anglo-puritan world would bring only benefit and salvation to them.

Her dream, which was common, was to have a piece of land, free of mortgage, with enough room for grapevines, gooseberries, strawberries, asparagus, and rhubarb, a garden, three peach trees, and an apple tree.

The design and beauty of this house moved me then, and when I see its abandoned replica on the plains, I weep. It was a haven against the wild menace of the time, a structural intensity promising only barest warmth, a Doric hearth, and a rigid, austere, expectant growth.

On the day of the opening of homesteading she got a corner lot, a small parcel of land she could register, and she built her wooden democratic temple upon it. The lot ran to what became an alley when the village was formally platted. The outhouse was on this alley. She had two cellars dug the first thing. The root cellar was half under the house, and the cyclone cellar, prepared at all times for disaster with blankets, food, and water, was separate from it. Once during a forest fire the cyclone cellar saved us from the smoke. Her dream, which was common, was to have a piece of land, free of mortgage, with enough room for grapevines, gooseberries, strawberries, asparagus, and rhubarb (all of which would return every year), a garden, three peach trees, and an apple tree. We had one milk cow freshening once a year, and one pig bought from a spring litter. The pig would fatten on our leavings by fall, and we would butcher him, smoke the hams and bacon, and render the lard for the year's frying. Even in a bad year we were almost independent. We had to buy (or exchange work or produce for) only kerosene, wood, coffee, and flour, although we could make flour from acorns or our own corn or, like Zona, from the cattails that grew in the swamp. Zona also ate young cattail shoots in spring salad.

The basement was under only part of the house and was lined with river stone, which made a foot-high base for the house—the yellow sandstone, as I saw it years later, remained strong and faithful. The pine boards also were still aligned straight in their naive simplicity and symmetry, the center holding, the beams holding, the floor hardly warped or slanting. The house was earnestly made with a sturdy belief that it was built to last for a hundred years at the least and to give hearth and ceiling and walls for earnest, simple people who did not ask too much. It contained not one piece of wasted wood or embellishment; it was made to hold the weather out and to hold the faithful human for a century within its piney undecorated wood, straight-angled at the corners, the strong hide of wood stretched to its utmost to protect us. It displayed only two indulgences. One was a little bay window, not rich or ostentatious, projecting barely enough to permit a table or a desk in the alcove; from the window I could look down two streets. I had my desk there and wrote my first stories there. The other indulgence was the front door with its clusters of acorn carvings that had been painted black or had turned black.

The first front room was the parlor, which was used only for company. The blinds were always drawn in the parlor to keep the big red roses in the rug from fading, and on two easels were lithographs of my grandmother's father and mother. The room opening off the parlor was the sitting room, and from there the large kitchen extended under the peach trees. We mainly lived in the kitchen with its big wood-burning stove in front of which we took our Saturday night baths in the washtub. My brothers and I bathed in the same water because we had to carry it from the pump, which was outside, or from the rain barrel, which stood under the eaves. I envied those who had indoor cisterns in which the rain water could accumulate and be pumped directly into the sink.

Through a passageway half open to the weather was the summer kitchen and the little room called the birthing room. In the summer people who had the money to buy "Mr. Rockefeller's kerosene" cooked in their summer kitchen and did not have to heat up the house or waste wood. (My grandmother always said, "Mr. Rockefeller's kerosene has gone up two cents. If it goes up any more to add to his wealth, we'll have to use candles!") Another small room off the kitchen was the only bedroom. My brothers and I slept in the sitting room on couches.

Perhaps another small indulgence was the narrow wooden porch that went one-third of the way around the front of the house, upheld by small handmade wooden pillars. Later we had a sidewalk in front of the house.

This type of house, found all over the Midwest prairies, is a cultural wonder expressing the clean, rudimentary, sober symmetry of the pioneer's needs and speaking of the builders and their materials. Expressing the solid duty of worker and timber and time—earnest, rigid, no fooling, no laxness, spare as the puritan world. The extension of my grandmother's skeleton, of her needs: of her rebuke to the sensuality and wildness of the frontier, faithful to a vengeful god, severe but just of her rebuke to the sensual stridency of violence and rowdiness. Single-handed in her long skirts and modesty— she never saw her own naked body bathing under that shift—she remarked in time and space of decency, uprightness, and duty. In her pure cabin she took the Ahabs back from their journeys. She cured the mad-drunk crew of beriberi and brought them back to the church altar and the brotherhood of Jesus.

This type of house, found all over the Midwest prairies, is a cultural wonder expressing the clean, rudimentary, sober symmetry of the pioneer's needs and speaking of the builders and their materials.

Inside we had my aunt's mission furniture, a style that had been fashionable but then had given way to antiques, so that the poor relatives got the heavy chairs covered in imitation leather. In the spaces of that house I worshipped. I heard my first music in the evening as my grandmother sat at the little foot-pumped organ and sang the only songs she knew, in the homely voice the puritan women seemed to have, as if a joyful or immense tone might be excessive. At church the cords of her neck always swelled out painfully and the sound was painful, of sorrow and asking, and preparation to cross over the river Jordan into the heavenly land. Lead us home, take our hands and lead us out of the wilderness, let us rest in thee. Horrors were sung about rugged and lonely wilds: day after day I plot and moil, sorrow in my troubled glimmering breast, death shining in the dark mysteries beyond my dust, stars in gloomy graves glow and glitter, let me walk in the air of glory, this is where we were crucified, this tree, this agonizing light, and the flowers blanched by fear, poor I pine, what hidden place conceals thee? And she sang her only love song, "Jesus, Lover of My Soul, Let Me to Thy Bosom Fly."

Only through these songs did I know the depths of her sorrow, her terrible loneliness, her wish to die, her deep silence. Sometimes I heard her cry in the night, but I could not humiliate her by going to comfort her. In the day there would be no sign. In abrasive irony she would fulfill the duties inside the shell of her devotion, this fragile house flung up in tepee-curled light by the sound of hammers where a nail had not been known, this puritan citadel, fragile yet strong, a psychic mansion, a fragment of hope and despair. We crouched in an alien land under the weathers, tossing at night on this ancient sea, captained by women, minute against the great white whale.

These houses still gleam empty on the prairies, the same houses from the same puritan, democratic dream, lost and lost again as my grandmother's house was lost in the depression before World War I. They still live in the minds of those fled to the cities or to battlefields in strange villages. This small enduring white frame house is in nightmare and terrible dream proliferated, floating in the flood of time. Let yourself down, as if under water, into these lost walls, to hunt for treasure, to illuminate violence with meaning. Under sea-strange light these little houses glimmer in memory, powerful as radium.

In that little wooden nutmeg of a house my grandmother's mind was full of angels, the last supper, and Mary's ascension into heaven. We were together in the vengeful wilderness with a vengeful god. We read the psalms and the resurrection of Jesus and the women at the tomb that morning of his rising. She waited to go to heaven. She thought she would and so would all those she loved. This world was run by the devil.

The frontier was a hard place to hold up the Christian virtues single-handedly, in fichus of crochet, corsets, gloves, and hats and covered to the ankle by long skirts. She had a big iron rod up her spine and a small one in her curled ironic lip when she at last was released from hell at eighty-five.

After World War II I went out to the prairies to look for my grandmother's house. It was still there in the village that had changed to an industrial center. I followed the sun on my shoulder to find the street. The house still drew me with its light and shine. There was the wide street, the corner house. It had been painted white not long before by some faithful Protestant, and the little front porch was still supported by the undecorated pillars holding up the staunch and unslanting room. The bay window was still there. The back porch even had the same lattice, though the roses had died out. The faithful lilac bush was uncut, frowsy but still there,

and the little irises still grew by the river stones that held up the house soberly and straight. The grape arbor had returned to wild grapes. One peach tree remained, spread out like an old matron, and I am sure in season bearing some kind of peaches. The people living in the house had had a hard time. The steps to the cellars were littered with whiskey bottles and coke bottles. A beheaded doll lay by the cyclone cellar. But repairs had been made, and a toilet had been added in one of the closets when the village had gotten water mains. The grass had held well, and I could even see some lilies of the valley near the back door.

When the front door was opened, I entered fearfully, the spaces of my girlhood still curving around me. Grandma's tall figure seemed to be about to appear in the doorway, her long arms under her apron. You see, she would be saying, I built a good house. Yes, I said, the floors even are not slanting: you built it solid.

The walls had been repapered time and again. It was wonderful and strange again to be inside the safe little square box. Not only the wood but the spirit of our flesh and all the harried flesh of a century now moved inside the snail shell, leaving the marks of movement intimate as marrow. I could see how the generations had made jelly from the grapes and had painted the good skeleton bright colors, the essential strength of my grandmother's being carrying her memory in this beautiful Doric shell.

Our fragility turns out to be strength. That sacred house seemed sunbonneted like my grandmother, spare and virginal. It had survived, as we have, the holocaust of our time, the human cyclone, and the hostilities of mid-America.

When we drove away, I didn't need to look back. That Pandora's box house had opened inside me, aswarm with apocalyptic light.

"THE PASSING OF THE OLD WEST"
Flocks of birds fly south above the ghost of a prairie farm in this painting by artist Francis Lee Jaques. Born in Illinois, Jaques found his home in Minnesota. Among his numerous paintings and ink drawings, he and his wife, Florence Page Jaques, collaborated on the book Canoe Country. *Jaques also illustrated birding guides and several of Sigurd Olson's classic books, including* Listening Point, The Singing Wilderness, *and* The Lonely Land. *(James Ford Bell Museum of Natural History)*

Culture Clash

By Jim Northrup

Jim Northrup is a natural storyteller. He has been telling tales all of his life, chronicling his roots, his stint in the Marine Corps in the Vietnam War, and his unique view of modern American and Native American culture. His candor, wry humor, and down-to-earth observations have won him readers throughout the country.

An Anishinaabe from the Fond du Lac Reservation, at the age of six he was ordered to attend a federal boarding school far away from his family; for secondary education, he was sent to a Christian boarding school in Hot Springs, South Dakota. With his wife Pat and their family, he now lives the traditional life of the Anishinaabe on Fond du Lac.

Northrup's first book of poems and short stories, *Walking the Rez Road*, was published by Voyageur Press in 1993. It collected together many of the stories that Northrup has been telling for decades around campfires, at powwows, and during wild rice harvest. The book won a Minnesota Book Award and a Northeast Minnesota Book Award.

Northrup is well known—or at least infamous—for his syndicated "Fond du Lac Follies" column that appears in the *Circle*, *Native American Press*, and *News From Indian Country*. In addition, his play "Shinnob Jep" was performed in October 1997 at the Weisman Art Museum as part of an Indian Humor exhibition. His most recent book is *The Rez Road Follies* (1997).

This piece from *Walking the Rez Road* is classic Northrup—a blend of irony, biting humor, social commentary, and picaresque adventure all rolled into one jewel of a story. His autobiographical hero Luke Warmwater is a Don Quixote in worn blue jeans, a ribbon shirt, and braids, tilting at the windmills of modern civilization.

MEETING OF CULTURES
Crown Princess Mary Dury and William Little Wolf meet at Itasca in 1949 to celebrate the Minnesota Territorial Centennial. (Minnesota Historical Society)

LUKE WARMWATER AND his old lady Dolly were riding down a gravel road on the reservation. Luke and Dolly were on a ride because they had the gas.

It was ricing season, but the lakes were closed so they could rest. The wind was combing the tangles out of the rice. They were glad because they knew they could harvest the next day.

Down the road they saw someone shambling along.

"A way day," said Luke, pointing with his lower lip.

"Ayah," agreed Dolly. "That's your brother, the one they call Almost, isn't it?"

"Yah, I wonder what the hell he's doing around here," wondered Luke.

From the way he walked, Luke knew Almost had been on a drunk. There was nothing unusual about that. What was unusual was the bloody washrag he held against his head.

Almost got into the car and said, "Hey, brother, you got a smoke?"

As Luke handed him one, he began complaining and explaining. He was complaining about the cut on his head and explaining how it happened.

"This gash must need thirty-seven stitches. How about a ride to the hospital?" Almost said.

"No problem," said Luke, "put your seatbelt on—we're now riding in an ambulance."

"That old girl broke her frying pan over my head, you know, one of those cast iron ones. I knew I shouldn't have gone home yet," Almost moaned. "Sure, I've been on a drunk, but she was laying for me when I got home. She used that frying pan for something besides fry bread."

"We went ricing yesterday," Luke said.

"That honk on the noggin did nothing to improve my hangover. She was yelling about that skinny Red Laker I

passed out next to. I got out of there before she really got mad," Almost continued.

"We got 150 pounds of rice at Dead Fish Lake yesterday," Luke said.

He began the ritual of "Rushing Him to the Hospital." He felt good about driving so fast. He was on a genuine mission of mercy and he could bend and even break the traffic laws.

Luke's old car was holding up pretty good on the high speed run. "She'll need a quart of oil by the time we get there," he said.

The cops sitting at the edge of town eating donuts didn't know of Luke's mission of mercy. All they saw was a carload of Indians weaving through traffic.

Donuts and curses flew through the air as they began one of their own institutions called "High Speed Chase."

One cop was screaming on the radio about the chase. The other was trying to keep track of all the laws that were being broken.

"Hey, all right, we got an official police escort," said Luke when he saw the red lights in his mirrors.

By this time Luke's escort had grown to three city squads, and deputies were coming to join the chase.

The ambulance came sliding into the hospital parking lot and stopped by the emergency room. Dolly got Almost out of the car and helped him into the building.

Luke drove over to where you're supposed to park and began congratulating himself on the successful run to the hospital. His troubles began when the cops got to the parking lot. They were excited about the chase.

"What's wrong with you, driving like that?" yelled a cop as he came running up to Luke.

"I wanna see your license!" screamed the second cop as he tried to wrestle Luke to the ground.

"Good, he's gonna resist arrest," said the first cop as he drew out his nightstick.

"My brother, Almost, is . . . ," Luke got out before a nightstick glanced off the side of his head and shut him up.

Luke gave up trying to explain and just began to fight back. He was holding his own and even took one of the nightsticks away. He threw that thing up on the roof so they'd quit hitting him with it.

The balance of power shifted towards the law and order as more cops piled into the battle. Pretty soon Luke was sitting on the pavement, a subdued and handcuffed Indian. There never is an easy way to end these things, he thought.

The cops jerked Luke up on his tiptoes and marched him into the emergency room. Luke's head needed some doctor attention after all those nightsticks. They laid Luke down on the table next to Almost.

ABOVE: **Powwow**

From his roots in Minneapolis, photographer William Albert Allard has gone on to cover the world with his camera. He studied at the University of Minnesota's journalism school and became obsessed with the classic 1930s documentary Let Us Now Praise Famous Men, *which blended the photos of Walker Evans with James Agee's prose. Going to work for* National Geographic, *Allard created famous photo essays focusing on American cowboys, farm laborers in the Mississippi Delta, the Amish of Lancaster County, and more. His most recent book,* Time at the Lake, *returns to Minnesota and a portrayal of the land of ten thousand lakes. This image captures the colors of a powwow at Cass Lake in 1991.*
(Photograph © William Albert Allard)

OPPOSITE PAGE: **Anishinaabe moccasins**

Anishinaabe artist Ellen B. Olson of Grand Portage crafted this pair of moccasins following ancient Ojibwe style. The moccasins are made from deer skin, and feature black velvet on the uppers and vamps. The Anishinaabe have long been famed for their fine beadwork, and these moccasins are ornamented with beaded floral and vine patterns.

"Matching stitches," growled Luke to his brother.

"Anin da nab," said Almost and then shut up when he saw the cops and cuffs.

There was something ironic about the whole situation, but Luke couldn't figure it out as the doctor stitched the brothers up.

The cops took Luke to jail. On the ride, Luke saw the ripped uniforms and lumps on the cops. That would explain why they put the cuffs on so damned tight.

Luke was pushed into his usual cellblock and he checked himself for damages. It was good to get those cuffs off.

A cop came in and handed Luke his copy of the charges. In addition to traffic charges, there was one for theft of city property. They couldn't find the nightstick he threw away.

The cellblock door clanged open and Almost was pushed in.

"We gotta stop meeting like this," sighed Luke. "What they got you for?"

"Disorderly conduct, and of course resisting arrest," said Almost.

"We'll go to court this afternoon," calculated Luke.

"When I got out of the hospital, the cops were still outside. They must have been mad yet because when I offered to drive your car home, they attacked," said Almost as he rubbed his cuff-damaged wrists.

So Almost went to jail, the car went with the tow truck, and Dolly went visiting relatives to raise bail money.

She got back to the jail as the brothers were being taken to court.

"Got you covered," she said as she flashed the bail money.

Luke grinned hard at her.

In court, the brothers Warmwater pleaded not guilty and demanded a jury trial. A new court date was set and the matter of bail came up.

Luke got up and addressed the judge.

"Your honor, I hate seeing you under these conditions. I've been here before and as you may recall, I've always showed up on time for court.

"Ricing comes only once a year. The harvest is good this year and my old lady, Dolly, is finally learning how to make rice. I'm sure you know how important to the Indian people the rice crop is.

"The reason I'm telling you all this is because I'd like to request a release on my own recognizance."

"Request granted," the judge said as he gaveled the case down the court calendar.

As long as he had the judge's ear, Luke got brave and said, "Oh, yeah, your honor, all that stuff is true for my brother too."

The judge cut them both loose. They walked out of there free ricing Indians. They used the bail money Dolly raised to rescue the car and to buy that quart of oil they needed.

They dropped Almost off at home. His old lady was kind of sorry about hitting him. When he promised to buy her a new frying pan, she forgave him. They began making preparations for ricing the next day.

Luke and Dolly continued their ride down the gravel road on the Reservation. Down the road, they saw someone walking.

"A way day," said Luke, pointing with his lower lip.

"Don't you dare stop, Luke Warmwater!" said Dolly.

OPPOSITE PAGE: "MUSIC TO MY EARS"
Anishinaabe artist Jeffrey Chapman's watercolor paintings blend past and present images to create a startling vision of modern Native American culture.

RIGHT: FRANCES DENSMORE AND RED FOX
Anshinaabe Chief Red Fox sings into a phonograph for folklorist Frances Densmore in Minneapolis in 1919. Densmore traveled much of the northwoods collecting stories, songs, and music of Native Americans, which she published in numerous books and Smithsonian Institution bulletins, including Chippewa Customs *(1929), and a long series on the music of numerous tribes. Her work survives today as a priceless record.* (Special Collections/Minneapolis Public Library)

A Choice of Weapons

By Gordon Parks

Music, writing, art, film, and photography—Gordon Parks has used all of these "weapons" during his life in his never-ending battle against racism.

Born in Kansas in 1912, Parks was orphaned at age sixteen and sent to live with relatives in St. Paul. He immediately ran away from an abusive brother-in-law and was forced to make his way on his own, attending high school, while sleeping nights in poolhalls and flophouses; hustling meals; hoboing and thumbing around the Midwest in search of jobs; playing piano in a brothel; waiting tables at the St. Paul Hotel; and lighting cigars for the rich and famous at the Minnesota Club.

Parks soon left St. Paul, moving on to work as a railroad porter, professional basketball player, and jazz pianist. It was a secondhand camera that finally gave him his chance. Inspired by photographers Dorothea Lange, John Vachon, and Walker Evans, Parks documented poverty among blacks on Chicago's South Side, images that won him respect and a step toward expressing himself beyond the reins of racism.

In addition to his photography for *Life* magazine, Parks was the author of several novels, including *The Learning Tree* (1963), and numerous musical compositions and films. In later years, Parks recorded his life in a series of memoirs, starting with *A Choice of Weapons* (1966), which chronicled his early years. His other autobiographies included *To Smile in Autumn* (1979) and

---

FROGTOWN

An African-American family gathers on its front porch in the Frogtown neighborhood of St. Paul. Chinese-American photographer Wing Young Huie was born and raised in Duluth, but he found his métier chronicling life in the inner city neighborhoods of the Twin Cities. His series of portraits of Frogtown won praise for Huie's passionate documentary eye. The images were displayed in a novel fashion in 1995— outdoors in a vacant lot along University Avenue; they were subsequently published in book form as Frogtown: Photographs and Conversations in an Urban Neighborhood. *(Photograph © Wing Young Huie)*

Voices in the Mirror (1990).

This excerpt from *A Choice of Weapons* portrays the young Parks as an Odysseus in a Minnesota winter in the 1930s, with the treasure at the end of his travels being a newfound understanding, resolve, and spirit to battle inequality.

MARCH CAME AND held at fifteen below for several days; then a warm front pushed in and brought relief. But a big snow followed. It started around eight one evening, and by the next morning the city was buried beneath its whiteness. Twenty-foot drifts blocked the highways. Stores and schools closed and nothing moved but snowplows and trolley cars. I borrowed a shovel from George and in two days I made over twenty-five dollars—enough to get a room for a month and a few meals. It was Friday when I moved into the rooming house, and I had bought a newspaper and gone to bed when I saw the ad. The Stumble Inn near Bemidji, Minnesota, wanted a piano player. The salary was eighteen dollars a week—and tips. The room and board were free and the hours from eight until two in the morning. I reasoned that I could stay in school with a job like that. I stood in the dimly lit room trying to decide. I had paid five dollars toward my rent, which I knew I couldn't get back. And it would mean leaving St. Paul. But the prospect of eating and sleeping regularly made it seem worthwhile. I got up, dressed, stuffed the paper in my pocket and hurried to the Western Union office.

My telegram naïvely advised that I would take the job and they could expect me within two days. And at six the next morning I was at the outskirts of town trying to thumb a ride to Bemidji. Car after car passed; and I stamped about in the snow trying to kill the numbness in my feet. The cold wind rose and began to whip fright into me and I was ready to turn back when a big truck slid to a stop. I jumped up on the running board, but my hands were too cold to turn the handle. The driver leaned over and opened the door and I jumped up into the cab.

"Where you headin'?" His accent was Southern.

"Bemidji."

"You're lucky. Goin' within fifteen miles of it."

We rode the next few miles in silence. Now and then he would curse the drifts as we approached them, gun his motor and burst through, sending flurries in every direction.

> *The cold wind rose and began to whip fright into me and I was ready to turn back when a big truck slid to a stop. I jumped up on the running board, but my hands were too cold to turn the handle. The driver leaned over and opened the door and I jumped up into the cab.*

The silences were awkward and I finally told him I was glad that he had picked me up.

"It's okay," he drawled, "'cause I git sleepy on long hauls. A little comp'ny keeps me goin'." Another drift was coming up. "Damn useless snow! I cain't see why people settle in ass-freezin' country like this anyhow. Cain't figger it out." We plowed through and snow shot high above the cab, blinding us for a moment or so—then the road was before us again.

I wanted to ask him where he came from, but he was a white Southerner and this might have led to some uncomfortable North-South talk. He had done me a big favor, and I was in no position to argue in case his views opposed mine—and I was sure they did. Then, as if he were clairvoyant, "I got a boy 'bout your size back in Florida, and I bet you a hound's tooth to a dollar he's lazyin' 'neath a orange tree in the back yard."

"He's lucky," I said.

"Maybe yes. Maybe no." I didn't know how to take that, so I kept quiet, waiting, so that he might clarify himself. "He ain't exactly a good boy, and he ain't exactly a bad one. Main thing wrong is he's got a lot of screwed-up ideas."

"Like what?"

"Well, he got us into a peck of trouble 'bout a week ago. We ain't out of it yet. It's not that my wife and me is against you people, but there's a time and place for everything. Well, my boy he gives a birthday party last week, and right in the middle of it a nigra boy who he invited walks smack through the front door, and my boy starts feedin' him cake and ice cream. Well, you don't know the commotion it started."

"What happened?"

"One of my boy's pals called him a nigga, and my boy hit him for doin' it. His own friend, mind you. Now every white boy in town wants to beat up on him. He's got hisself in a peck of trouble. He should never done such a thing in the first place. You think so?"

"I don't know."

"Would your paw like it if you invited a white boy to your birthday party? "

"I never had a birthday party."

"But s'pose you did . . . you think he'd like it?"

"He wouldn't care one bit."

"How do you know if you never had a birthday party?"

"I just know my poppa, that's all."

"Well, what you are saying is my boy don't know me."

"I didn't say that."

We were silent for some time after that. His manner told me he was thinking deeply. "You ever sleep with a white girl, boy?"

"Did you ever sleep with a colored girl? "

"Yeh, I did. And it was good. Now how 'bout you?"

I stiffened and got ready to thumb the rest of the way to Bemidji. "Yessir, I have," I lied, "and it wasn't so good."

To my surprise he roared with laughter. "Just wait till my boy hears what you said. It'll kill him. By god, it'll kill him." He continued laughing for almost another mile. After that I went to sleep, deeply puzzled by his reaction.

Sometime later in the night he nudged me in the ribs. "I quit you here. Bemidji's about fifteen miles down the road. Market trucks'll be goin' in for the weekend. You oughta git a lift 'fore long."

I rubbed sleep from my eyes and peered out. The highway marker, caught in the glare of the headlights, fixed my destination as exactly fifteen and a half miles. I thanked him and jumped down to the snowbank. As the truck roared off, I watched the whiteness swirl upward and around it obscuring the only thing moving through the blackness. The sound of the motor gradually faded, and I turned and started down the road. The wind had died, but the temperature this far north was still far below zero. Past Kansas winters had taught me in such instances to keep moving, not too fast, not too slow—just enough, as my dad used to warn, to keep the blood running hot. A few market trucks did come along, but they didn't stop, and I made the whole distance on foot, reaching the outskirts a little after one o'clock in the morning. I saw a garage and stopped there to get warm.

The white garage keeper was kind. He gave me a cheese sandwich and three cups of coffee and, as I sat in the heat of his pot-bellied stove, I remarked that it was the same type as we had back in Kansas. He asked me where I was going, and I proudly mentioned the job I had come to take at Stumble Inn.

"When you starting?"

"Soon as I can find the place."

"Why, didn't you come down the main road?"

"That's right."

"Good Lord, fellow, you passed it about three and a half miles back." My expression must have been most lamentable, for he immediately asked me if I would like to sleep there until morning. Wearily I accepted. There were two bales of

Momma used to say that strength came through prayer. I prayed these nights, but I was beginning to wonder about a God who would test me so severely.

hay in the corner, and I collapsed on them. The garage keeper threw me a horse blanket. I covered myself with it and slept as soundly as I had ever slept in my life.

As far as the owner of Stumble Inn was concerned, I could have remained in the garage forever. When I knocked at his place the next morning, he came to the door in his long underwear. I had awakened him and he regarded me impatiently as I explained who I was. "Hell," he said, "that job's already taken." Then he slammed the door in my face.

I went back to town and looked about for work all day, without success. By eleven o'clock that night a blizzard raged. The streets were deserted. I went back to the garage, but it was closed. Through the driving snow I saw a lighted sign that said eat. Already weak, I felt faint as I was pushed along by the strong gusts. I reached the door and went inside.

"What do you want?" the waitress asked.

"A cup of coffee," I said, then I collapsed on a stool. Three white men and a woman sat at a table alongside the wall. They had been drinking. "Well, ah declare!" one of the men said in a heavy Southern drawl. "Ah seen eva'thing now. A nigga eatin' in the very same place as white folks. Ain't nothin' gonna happen like that down where ah come from."

I ignored him. He went on. "Black bastards'll be wantin' to git in our beds next!"

Suddenly my control was gone. I grabbed my cup and dashed the scalding coffee on him. He yelled. The woman next to him screamed. I began throwing sugar bowls, salt and pepper shakers, ketchup bottles, anything that I could get my hands on.

All at once the waitress shouted a warning, but it was too late. A chair knocked me unconscious. I came to while being hauled from the diner by two policemen. They took me to jail.

When they released me from jail the following morning, there was a soreness where the chair had struck my temple. The day was cold but clear, and I started walking toward the highway. As I passed the cafe, it appeared innocent of the violence that had erupted there only a few hours before. It was like passing a tombstone one had defaced, and I hurried on. Soon Bemidji and Stumble Inn were far behind me, and two hours later I was picked up by another trucker. Luck was with me. He was going all the way to St. Paul. It was easier to relax now, for I would be back in time for school on Monday morning, and I had a room—for at least the rest of the month.

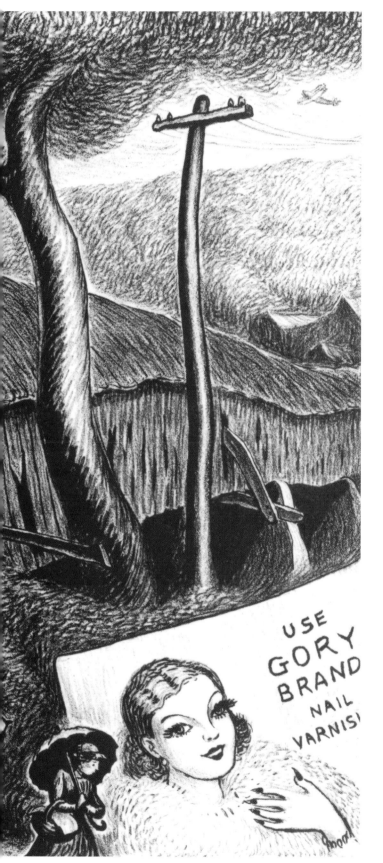

As the truck bumped over the highway, I thought back over the fruitless journey. I couldn't understand that Southern truck driver. Had he picked me up out of kindness, or was he trying to expiate his feeling about Negroes? Why, after asking such a question, had he roared with laughter at my flippant answer? Was he trying to understand his own son through me, or maybe understand me through his son? I didn't know. It was impossible to judge him in terms of his actions. Then there were the garage man and the innkeeper, both white, but as different as summer and winter. Next, the other Southerner with whom I had fought in the cafe. He had obviously deserved his lumps. But had I handled that situation the way my mother would have wanted me to? No, she would have found some other way to defeat him and yet maintain her dignity and pride. But this man's tongue had hurt worse than a fist, and I had reacted out of an impulse fed by despair. My conscience told me that my actions were wrong, but my heart approved them. Momma used to say that strength came through prayer. I prayed these nights, but I was beginning to wonder about a God who would test me so severely.

I had come north to prove my worth, and I was discovering that there was a lot more to it than just the desire for recognition or success. The naïveté of youth, the frustrations of being black had me trapped, and achievement seemed almost impossible. It was becoming more and more difficult to live with the indifference, the hate, and at the same time endure the poverty. But even then I knew I couldn't go on feeling condemned because of my color. I made up my mind, there in the cab of that truck, that I wouldn't allow my life to be conditioned by what others thought or did, or give in to anyone who would have me be subservient. We rolled into St. Paul about three in the morning. The disappointing trip had left me tired and wounded; I was glad to be back.

"PROGRESS"

Wanda Gág's life story is often compared to that of Cinderella. Born in poverty in New Ulm, she made a name for herself as an illustrator and artist. In 1928, her masterpiece children's book Millions of Cats *was published, winning the prestigious Newberry Honor Award and finding its way into the hearts of children for generations. Gág also illustrated numerous other children's books as well as creating other works of art, including this 1936 lithograph showing all the signs of progress along a country road. (Minnesota Historical Society)*

CHAPTER TWO

NORTH OF EDEN

"The fact is that most country or small-town Minnesotans love snow.
They relish snow in large inconvenient storms; they like the excesses of it,
they like the threat of it, the endless work of it, the glamour of it."
—Carol Bly, *Letters From the Country*, 1981

Despite towns boasting names like Belle Prairie, Harmony, and Evergreen, Minnesota is a long way north of Eden. For many Native Americans and immigrants, however, the state was truly a promised land despite the climate. These excerpts and essays tell of the hardships and values of life this side of paradise.

ABOVE: A FINE DAY OF FISHING
Two proud anglers congratulate each other on their catch. The fisherman were photographed in Stillwater in 1913 by Stillwater commercial photographer John Runk. (Minnesota Historical Society)

OPPOSITE: ICE
This abstract image of ice shards at Shovel Point in Tettegouche State Park comes from Craig Blacklock's album Lake Superior Images *(1993). Nature photographer Blacklock hails from a family dynasty renowned for its photographic vision of the outdoors. Craig's father Les began photographing Minnesota decades ago, first publishing his images of the state in book form in* Meet My Psychiatrist, *published by Voyageur Press in 1977. Since then, Les, his wife Fran, son Craig, and Craig's wife Nadine collaborated on numerous books and calendars focused on the natural beauty of Minnesota, including* Minnesota Wild *and* Our Minnesota, *both published by Voyageur Press.* (Photograph © Craig Blacklock)

The Glittering Cloud

By Laura Ingalls Wilder

Laura Ingalls Wilder lived the life she wrote of in her numerous volumes chronicling pioneer days. Her books offer a detailed and honest portrayal of the ways of the settlers. It is for that reason—and for the colorful anecdotes of the young Laura—that they have been read by generations of children and adults.

Laura Elizabeth Ingalls was born in 1867 in a log house in the Wisconsin Big Woods. During her childhood, she traveled west by covered wagon to Indian Territory in Kansas and then on to Minnesota, where her family finally settled.

In later years, Wilder told stories of her pioneer days to her own daughter, Rose, who urged her mother to write the stories down for posterity. Her first book, *Little House in the Big Woods* (1932), covered the years 1871 and 1872, when Laura was four and five years old. Subsequent books in the series included *Little House on the Prairie* (1935), *On the Banks of Plum Creek* (1937), *By the Shores of Silver Lake* (1939), *The Long Winter* (1940), *Little Town on the Prairie* (1941), *These Happy Golden Years* (1943). Wilder also authored other books and series.

This chapter from *On the Banks of Plum Creek* tells of Laura's family's early days in Minnesota, the hard winters, and the dreadful grasshopper plague.

HOME SWEET SOD HOME

Many a Minnesota farmstead began with a sod house. Pioneers coming west dug up the earth and stacked the "bricks" of sod to create the walls of a home that often housed the family for years, if not decades. As Ole Rölvaag wrote in Giants in the Earth, *"He was building a sod house. The walls had now risen breast-high; in its half-finished condition, the structure resembled more a bulwark against some enemy than anything intended to be a human habitation. And the great heaps of cut sod, piled up in each corner, might well have been the stores of ammunition for defense of the stronghold." This sod house in Sanborn still stands, speaking of the inherent suitability of such structures for the Minnesota prairie. (Photograph © Richard Hamilton Smith)*

Now THE WHEAT was almost ready to cut.

Every day Pa looked at it. Every night he talked about it, and showed Laura some long, stiff wheat-heads. The plump grains were getting harder in their little husks. Pa said the weather was perfect for ripening wheat.

"If this keeps up," he said, "We'll start harvesting next week."

The weather was very hot. The thin, high sky was too hot to look at. Air rose up in waves from the whole prairie, as it does from a hot stove. In the schoolhouse the children panted like lizards, and the sticky pine-juice dripped down the board walls.

Saturday morning Laura went walking with Pa to look at the wheat. It was almost as tall as Pa. He lifted her onto his shoulder so that she could see over the heavy, bending tops. The field was greeny gold.

At the dinner table Pa told Ma about it. He had never seen such a crop. There were forty bushels to the acre, and wheat was a dollar a bushel. They were rich now. This was a wonderful country. Now they could have anything they wanted. Laura listened and thought, now Pa would get his new boots.

She sat facing the open door and the sunshine streaming through it. Something seemed to dim the sunshine. Laura rubbed her eyes and looked again. The sunshine really was dim. It grew dimmer until there was no sunshine.

"I do believe a storm is coming up," said Ma. "There must be a cloud over the sun."

Pa got up quickly and went to the door. A storm might hurt the wheat. He looked out, then he went out.

The light was queer. It was not like the changed light before a storm. The air did not press down as it did before a storm. Laura was frightened, she did not know why.

She ran outdoors, where Pa stood looking up at the sky. Ma and Mary came out, too, and Pa asked, "What do you make of that, Caroline?"

A cloud was over the sun. It was not like any cloud they had ever seen before. It was a cloud of something like snow-flakes, but they were larger than snowflakes, and thin and glittering. Light shone through each flickering particle.

There was no wind. The grasses were still and the hot air did not stir, but the edge of the cloud came on across the sky faster than wind. The hair stood up on Jack's neck. All at once he made a frightful sound up at that cloud, a growl and a whine.

Plunk! something hit Laura's head and fell to the ground. She looked down and saw the largest grasshopper she had ever seen. Then huge brown grasshoppers were hitting the ground all around her, hitting her head and her face and her arms. They came thudding down like hail.

The cloud was hailing grasshoppers. The cloud *was* grasshoppers. Their bodies hid the sun and made darkness. Their thin, large wings gleamed and glittered. The rasping whirring of their wings filled the whole air and they hit the ground and the house with the noise of a hailstorm.

Laura tried to beat them off. Their claws clung to her skin and her dress. They looked at her with bulging eyes, turning their heads this way and that. Mary ran screaming into the house. Grasshoppers covered the ground, there was not one bare bit to step on. Laura had to step on grasshoppers and they smashed squirming and slimy under her feet.

Ma was slamming the windows shut, all around the house. Pa came and stood just inside the front door, looking out. Laura and Jack stood close beside him. Grasshoppers beat down from the sky and swarmed thick over the ground. Their long wings were folded and their strong legs took them hopping everywhere. The air whirred and the roof went on sounding like a roof in a hailstorm.

Then Laura heard another sound, one big sound made of tiny nips and snips and gnawings.

"The wheat!" Pa shouted. He dashed out the back door and ran toward the wheat-field.

The grasshoppers were eating. You could not hear one grasshopper eat, unless you listened very carefully while you held him and fed him grass. Millions and millions of grasshoppers were eating now. You could hear the millions of jaws biting and chewing.

Pa came running back to the stable. Through the window Laura saw him hitching Sam and David to the wagon. He began pitching old dirty hay from the manure-pile into the wagon, as fast as he could. Ma ran out, took the other pitchfork and helped him. Then he drove away to the wheat-field and Ma followed the wagon.

Pa drove around the field, throwing out little piles of stuff as he went. Ma stooped over one, then a thread of smoke rose from it and spread. Ma lighted pile after pile. Laura watched till a smudge of smoke hid the field and Ma and Pa and the wagon.

Grasshoppers were still falling from the sky. The light was still dim because grasshoppers covered the sun.

Ma came back to the house, and in the closed lean-to she took off her dress and her petticoats and killed the grasshoppers she shook out of them. She had lighted fires all around the wheat-field. Perhaps smoke would keep the grasshoppers from eating the wheat.

Ma and Mary and Laura were quiet in the shut, smothery house. Carrie was so little that she cried, even in Ma's arms. She cried herself to sleep. Through the walls came the sound of grasshoppers eating.

The darkness went away. The sun shone again. All over

the ground was a crawling, hopping mass of grasshoppers. They were eating all the soft, short grass off the knoll. The tall prairie grasses swayed and bent and fell.

"Oh, look," Laura said, low, at the window.

They were eating the willow tops. The willows' leaves were thin and bare twigs stuck out. Then whole branches were bare, and knobby with masses of grasshoppers.

"I don't want to look any more," Mary said, and she went away from the window. Laura did not want to look any more, either, but she could not stop looking.

The hens were funny. The two hens and their gawky pullets were eating grasshoppers with all their might. They were used to stretching their necks out low and running fast after grasshoppers and not catching them. Every time they stretched out now, they got a grasshopper right then. They were surprised. They kept stretching out their necks and trying to run in all directions at once.

"Well, we won't have to buy feed for the hens," said Ma. "There's no great loss without some gain."

The green garden rows were wilting down. The potatoes, the carrots, the beets and beans were being eaten away. The long leaves were eaten off the cornstalks, and the tassels, and the ears of young corn in their green husks fell covered with grasshoppers.

There was nothing anybody could do about it.

Smoke still hid the wheat-field. Sometimes Laura saw Pa moving dimly in it. He stirred up the smouldering fires and thick smoke hid him again.

When it was time to go for Spot, Laura put on stockings and shoes and a shawl. Spot was standing in the old ford of Plum Creek, shaking her skin and switching her tail. The herd went mournfully lowing beyond the old dugout. Laura was sure that cattle could not eat grass so full of grasshoppers. If the grasshoppers ate all the grass, the cattle would starve.

Grasshoppers were thick under her petticoats and on her dress and shawl. She kept striking them off her face and hands. Her shoes and Spot's feet crunched grasshoppers.

Ma came out in a shawl to do the milking. Laura helped her. They could not keep grasshoppers out of the milk. Ma had brought a cloth to cover the pail but they could not keep it covered while they milked into it. Ma skimmed out the grasshoppers with a tin cup.

Grasshoppers went into the house with them. Their

HARVEST LUNCH
John A. Johnson and his family rest in the shade of a haystack for lunchtime during the harvest in Nicollet County in 1907. (Minnesota Historical Society)

THUNDERSTORM
Ominous clouds sweep over the prairie at Blue Mounds State Park in this image by landscape photographer Gary Alan Nelson. Based in Center City, Nelson has captured the spirit of the land in photographs that tell stories about a sense of place and history. (Photograph © Gary Alan Nelson)

clothes were full of grasshoppers. Some jumped onto the hot stove where Mary was starting supper. Ma covered the food till they had chased and smashed every grasshopper. She swept them up and shoveled them into the stove.

Pa came into the house long enough to eat supper while Sam and David were eating theirs. Ma did not ask him what was happening to the wheat. She only smiled and said: "Don't worry, Charles. We've always got along."

Pa's throat rasped and Ma said: "Have another cup of tea, Charles. It will help get the smoke out of your throat."

When Pa had drunk the tea, he went back to the wheat-field with another load of old hay and manure.

In bed, Laura and Mary could still hear the whirring and snipping and chewing. Laura felt claws crawling on her. There were no grasshoppers in bed, but she could not brush the feeling off her arms and cheeks. In the dark she saw grass-hoppers' bulging eyes and felt their claws crawling until she went to sleep.

Pa was not downstairs next morning. All night he had been working to keep the smoke over the wheat, and he did not come to breakfast. He was still working.

The whole prairie was changed. The grasses did not wave; they had fallen in ridges. The rising sun made all the prairie rough with shadows where the tall grasses had sunk against each other.

The willow trees were bare. In the plum thickets only a few plumpits hung to the leafless branches. The nipping, clicking, gnawing sound of the grasshoppers' eating was still going on.

At noon Pa came driving the wagon out of the smoke. He put Sam and David into the stable, and slowly came to the house. His face was black with smoke and his eyeballs were red. He hung his hat on the nail behind the door and sat down at the table.

"It's no use, Caroline," he said. "Smoke won't stop them. They keep dropping down through it and hopping in from all sides. The wheat is falling now. They're cutting it off like a scythe. And eating it, straw and all."

He put his elbows on the table and hid his face with his hands. Laura and Mary sat still. Only Carrie on her high stool rattled her spoon and reached her little hand toward the bread. She was too young to understand.

"Never mind, Charles," Ma said. "We've been through hard times before."

Laura looked down at Pa's patched boots under the table and her throat swelled and ached. Pa could not have new boots now.

Pa's hands came down from his face and he picked up his knife and fork. His beard smiled, but his eyes would not twinkle. They were dull and dim.

"Don't worry, Caroline," he said. "We did all we could, and we'll pull through somehow."

Then Laura remembered that the new house was not paid for. Pa had said he would pay for it when he harvested the wheat.

It was a quiet meal, and when it was over Pa lay down on the floor and went to sleep. Ma slipped a pillow under his head and laid her finger on her lips to tell Laura and Mary to be still.

They took Carrie into the bedroom and kept her quiet with their paper dolls. The only sound was the sound of the grasshoppers' eating.

Day after day the grasshoppers kept on eating. They ate all the wheat and the oats. They ate every green thing—all the garden and all the prairie grass.

"Oh, Pa, what will the rabbits do?" Laura asked. "And the poor birds? "

"Look around you, Laura," Pa said.

The rabbits had all gone away. The little birds of the grass tops were gone. The birds that were left were eating grass-hoppers. And prairie hens ran with outstretched necks, gob-bling grasshoppers.

When Sunday came, Pa and Laura and Mary walked to Sunday school. The sun shone so bright and hot that Ma said she would stay at home with Carrie, and Pa left Sam and David in the shady stable.

There had been no rain for so long that Laura walked across Plum Creek on dry stones. The whole prairie was bare and brown. Millions of brown grasshoppers whirred low over it. Not a green thing was in sight anywhere.

All the way, Laura and Mary brushed off grasshoppers. When they came to the church, brown grasshoppers were thick on their petticoats. They lifted their skirts and brushed them off before they went in. But careful as they were, the grasshoppers had spit tobacco-juice on their best Sunday dresses.

Nothing would take out the horrid stains. They would have to wear their best dresses with the brown spots on them.

Many people in town were going back East. Christy and Cassie had to go. Laura said good-bye to Christy and Mary said good-bye to Cassie, their best friends.

They did not go to school any more. They must save their shoes for winter and they could not bear to walk bare-footed on grasshoppers. School would be ended soon, any-way, and Ma said she would teach them through the winter so they would not be behind their classes when school opened again next spring.

Pa worked for Mr. Nelson and earned the use of Mr. Nelson's plough. He began to plough the bare wheat-field, to make it ready for next year's wheat crop.

The Heart That Dared Not Let in the Sun

By O. E. Rölvaag

Ole Edvart Rölvaag created a masterpiece with his novel *Giants in the Earth*, the chronicle of a Norwegian immigrant settlement on the Minnesota–South Dakota border. The book still stands today as a moving portrait of the hardships and joys of the pioneers' world—and as a chapter of Minnesota history.

Rölvaag himself emigrated from Norway in 1896, leaving behind the life of a fisherman for the promised land. He ventured to his uncle's farm in Elk Point, South Dakota, where he found work as a farmhand. In the coming years, he went on to study at St. Olaf College in Northfield, where he later became professor of Norwegian language and literature.

Even alongside other famous immigrant novels such as Johan Bojer's *The Emigrants* and Vilhelm Moberg's Swedish quartet, Rölvaag's epic trilogy remains the most enduring—and the most heartrending. His novels were unique in that he wrote many of them in Norwegian: the two books that make up *Giants in the Earth*—*I De Dage* ("In Those Days") and *Riket Grundlægges* ("Founding the Kingdom")—were originally published in Norway in 1924 and 1925. The novel was published in the United States in 1927 and became a bestseller.

Rölvaag's literary legacy was tied to the immigrant's story. His other works included *Pure Gold* (1930), originally published as *To Tullinger*, or "Two Fools," in 1920; *The Boat of Longing* (1933), originally published as *Længselens Baat* in 1922; and *The Third Life of Per Smevik* (1971), originally published as *Amerika-Breve*, or "Letters from America," in 1912. Rölvaag also wrote two novels that completed a trilogy started with *Giants in the Earth*: *Peder Victorious* (1929), originally published as *Peder Seier* in 1928; and *Their Father's God* (1931), originally published as

---

ABANDONED HOME
Once home to a family, a lonely farmstead house stands forsaken on the frozen prairie in Ottertail County. (Photograph © Gary Alan Nelson)

Den Signede Dag also in 1931.

In creating the immigrants Per and Beret Hansa of *Giants in the Earth*, Rölvaag wrote from personal experience. The section here is perhaps the most horrifying, telling of Beret's encroaching insanity in the world of all-encompassing whiteness that was the prairie winter.

THE DAYS WORE ON . . . sunny days . . . bleak, gloomy days, with cold that congealed all life.

There was one who heeded not the light of the day, whether it might be grey or golden. Beret stared at the earthen floor of the hut and saw only night round about her.

Yes . . . she faced only darkness. She tried hard, but she could not let in the sun.

Ever since she had come out here a grim conviction had been taking stronger and stronger hold on her. This was her retribution!

Now had fallen the punishment which the Lord God had meted out to her; at last His visitation had found her out and she must drink the cup of his wrath. Far away she had fled, from the rising of the sun to the going down thereof . . . so it had seemed to her . . . but the arm of His might had reached farther still. No, she could not escape—this was her retribution!

The stillness out here had given her full opportunity for reflection; all the fall she had done nothing but brood and remember. . . . Alas! she had much to remember!

She had accepted the hand of Per Hansa because she must—although no law had compelled her; she and he were the only people who had willed it thus. She had been gotten with child by him out of wedlock; nevertheless, no one had compelled her to marry him—neither father, nor mother, nor anyone in authority. It had been wholly her own doing. Her parents, in fact, had set themselves against the marriage with all their might, even after the child, Ole, had come.

. . . It had mattered nothing at all what they had said, nor what anyone else had said; for her there had been no other person in the world but Per Hansa! Whenever she had been with him she had forgotten the admonitions and prayers of her father and mother. . . . He had been life itself to her; without him there had been nothing. . . . Therefore she had given herself to him, although she had known it was a sin— had continued to give herself freely, in a spirit of abandoned joy.

Now she found plenty of time to remember how her parents had begged and threatened her to break with him;

Ever since she had come out here a grim conviction had been taking stronger and stronger hold on her. This was her retribution!

she recalled all that they had said, turning it over in her mind and examining it minutely. . . . Per Hansa was a shiftless fellow, they had told her; he drank; he fought; he was wild and reckless; he got himself tangled up in all sorts of brawls; no honourable woman could be happy with such a man. He probably had affairs with other women, too, whenever he had a chance. . . . All the other accusations she knew to be true; but not the last—no, not the last! She alone among women held his heart. The certainty of this fact had been the very sweetness of life to her. . . . What did she care for the rest of it! All was as nothing compared with this great certainty. . . . Ah, no—she knew it well enough: for him she was the only princess!

But now she understood clearly all that her parents had done to end it between them, and all the sacrifices they had been willing to make; she had not realized it at the time. . . . Oh, those kind-hearted parents on whom she had turned her back in order that she might cleave to him: how they must have suffered! The life which she and he had begotten in common guilt they had offered to take as their own, give it their name and their inheritance, and bring it up as their very child. They had freely offered to use their hard-earned savings to send her away from the scene of her shame . . . *so* precious had she been to them! But she had only said no, and no, and *no*, to all their offers of sacrifice and love! . . . Had there ever been a transgression so grievous as hers!

. . . Yet how could she ever have broken with him? Where Per Hansa was, there dwelt high summer and there it bloomed for her. How can a human forsake his very life? . . . Whenever she heard of one of his desperately reckless cruises through rough and stormy seas, on which he had played with the lives of his comrades as well as his own, her cheeks would glow and her heart would flame. This was the man her heart had chosen—this was he, and he alone! a voice would sing within her. Or when she sat among the heather on the mountain side in the fair summer night, and he came to her and laid his head in her lap—the tousled head that only she could lull to sleep—then she felt that now she was crossing the very threshold of paradise! . . . Though she had had a thousand lives, she would have thrown them all away for one such moment—and would have been glad of the bargain! . . .

. . . Yes, she remembered all that had happened in those days; it was so still out here . . . so easy to remember!

No one had ever told her, but she knew full well who it was that had persuaded Hans Olsa to leave the land and the ancient farm that had been in his family for generations, and go to America. There had been only one other person in the world whom Per Hansa loved, and that was Hans Olsa. She had been jealous of Hans Olsa because of this; it had seemed to her that he took something that rightfully belonged to her. She had even felt the same way toward Sörine, who was kindness itself; on this account she had not been able to hold her friendship as fully as she needed to, either in Norway or here. . . .

. . . But when Per Hansa had come home from Lofoten that spring and announced in his reckless, masterful way that he was off for America: would Beret come now, or wait until later? . . . Well, there hadn't been a "no" in her mouth then! There she had sat, with three children in a nice little home which, after the manner of simple folk, they had managed to build. . . . But she had risen up, taken the children with her, and left it all as if nothing mattered but him!

. . . How her mother had wept at that time! . . . How her father had grieved when they had left! Time after time he had come begging to Per Hansa, offering him all that he had— boat and fishing outfit, house and farm— if only he would settle down in Norway and not take their daughter from them forever. . . . But Per Hansa had laughed it all aside! There had been a power in his unflinching determination which had sent hot waves through her. She must have led a double life at that time; she had been sad with her parents but had rejoiced with Per Hansa. He had raged like a storm through those days, wild and reckless—and sometimes ruthless, too. . . . No!—he had cried— they would just make that little trip across the ocean! America—that's the country where a poor devil can get ahead! Besides, it was only a little way; if they didn't like it, they could drift back on the first fair western breeze! . . . So they had sold off everything that they had won with so much toil, had left it all like a pair of worn-out shoes—parents, home, fatherland, and people. . . . And she had done it gladly, even rejoicingly! . . . Was there ever a sin like hers?

. . . Then she had arrived in America. The country did not at all come up to her expectations; here, too, she saw enough of poverty and grinding toil. What did it avail, that the rich soil lay in endless stretches? More than ever did she realize that "man liveth not by bread alone!" . . . Even the bread was none too plentiful at times. . . .

Beyond a doubt, it was Destiny that had brought her thither. . . . Destiny, the inexorable law of life, which the Lord God from eternity had laid down for every human being, according to the path He knew would be taken. . . . Now

punishment stood here awaiting her—the punishment for having broken God's commandment of filial obedience. . . . Throughout the fall she had been reckoning up her score, and it came out exactly thus: Destiny had so arranged everything that the punishment should strike her all the more inevitably. Destiny had cast her into the arms of Per Hansa— and she did not regret it! Destiny had held up America as an enticing will-o'-the-wisp—and they had followed! . . .

But no sooner had they reached America than the west-fever had smitten the old settlements like a plague. Such a thing had never happened before in the history of mankind; people were intoxicated by bewildering visions; they spoke dazedly, as though under the force of a spell. . . . "Go west! . . . Go west, folks! . . . The farther west, the better the land!" . . . Men beheld in feverish dreams the endless plains, teeming with fruitfulness, glowing, out there where day sank into night—a Beulah Land of corn and wine! . . . She had never dreamed that the good Lord would let such folly loose among men. Were it only the young people who had been caught by the plague, she would not have wondered; but the old had been taken even worse. . . . "Now we're bound west!" said the young. . . . "Wait a minute—we're going along with you!" cried the old, and followed after. . . . Human beings gathered together, in small companies and large—took whatever was movable along, and left the old homestead without as much as a sigh! Ever westward led the course, to where the sun glowed in matchless glory as it sank at night; people drifted about in a sort of delirium, like sea birds in mating time; then they flew toward the sunset, in small flocks and large—always toward Sunset Land. . . . Now she saw it clearly: here on the trackless plains, the thousand-year-old hunger of the poor after human happiness had been unloosed!

Into this feverish atmosphere they had come. Could Destiny have spun his web more cunningly? She remembered well how the eyes of Per Hansa had immediately begun to gleam and glow! . . . And the strange thing about this spell had been that he had become so very kind under it. How playfully affectionate he had grown toward her during the last winter and spring! It had been even more deliciously sweet to give herself to him then, than back in those days when she had first won him. Was it not worth all the care and sorrow in the world to taste such bliss, she had often asked herself—but had been unable to answer. But—then it had happened: this spring she had been gotten with child again. . . . Let no one tell her that this was not Destiny!

She had urged against this last journey; she had argued that they must tarry where they were until she had borne the

. . . Then she had arrived in America. The country did not at all come up to her expectations; here, too, she saw enough of poverty and grinding toil.

child. One year more or less would make no difference, considering all the land there was in the west. . . . Hans Olsa, however, had been ready to start; and so there had been no use in trying to hold back Per Hansa. All her misgiving he had turned to sport and laughter, or playful love; he had embraced her, danced around with her, and become so roguish that she had been forced to laugh with him. . . . "Come here, *Litagod*—now we're gone!" . . . She well recalled how lovely this endearing term had sounded in her ears, the first night he had used it. . . .

But this was clear to her beyond a doubt: Per Hansa was without blame in what had happened—all the blame was hers. . . . He had never been so tender toward her as in the days since they had come out here; she could not have thought it possible for one human being to have such strong desire for another as he held. . . . Who could match him—who dared follow where he led? She remembered all that he had wrought since they had set out on their journey last spring, and felt that no one else could do it after him. He was like the north wind that sweeps the cloud banks from the heavens! . . . At these thoughts, something unspeakably soft and loving came into Beret's eyes. . . . No, not like the north wind: like the gentle breeze of a summer's nights—that's how he was! . . . And this, too, was only retribution! She had bound herself inseparably to this man; now she was but a hindrance to him, like chains around his feet: him, whom she loved unto madness, she burdened and impeded . . . she was only in his way!

. . . But that he could not understand it—that he could not fathom the source of her trouble; that seemed wholly incomprehensible to her. Didn't he realize that she could never be like him? . . . No one in all the world was like him! How could she be? . . .

Beret struggled with many thoughts these days.

. . . Wasn't it remarkable how ingeniously Destiny had arranged it all? For ten long years he had cast her about like a chip on the current, and then had finally washed her ashore here. *Here*, far off in the great stillness, where there was nothing to hide behind—here the punishment would fall! . . . Could a better place have been found in which to lay her low?

. . . Life was drawing to a close. One fact stood before her constantly: she would never rise again from the bed in which she was soon to lie down. . . . This was the end.

. . . Often, now, she found herself thinking of the churchyard at home. . . . It would have been so pleasant to lie down

there. . . . The churchyard was enclosed by a massive stone wall, broad and heavy; one couldn't imagine anything more reliable than that wall. She had sat on it often in the years when she was still her father's little girl. . . . In the midst of the churchyard lay the church, securely protecting everything round about. No fear had ever dwelt in that place; she could well remember how the boys used to jump over the graves; it had been great fun, too—at times she had joined the game. . . . Within that wall many of her dear ones slumbered: two brothers whom she had never seen, and a little sister that she remembered quite clearly, though she had died long, long ago; her grandparents, on both her father's and her mother's side, also rested here, and one of her great-grandfathers. She knew where all these graves lay. Her whole family, generation after generation, rested there—many more than she had any knowledge of. . . . Around the churchyard stood a row of venerable trees, looking silently down on the peace and the stillness within. . . . They gave such good shelter, those old trees!

. . . She could not imagine where he would bury her out here. . . . *Now*, in the dead of winter—the ground frozen hard! . . . How would he go about it? . . . If he would. Only dig deep down . . . the wolves gave such unearthly howls at night! No matter what he thought of it, she would have to speak to him about the grave. . . . Well, no need to mention it just now.

One day when Beret had to go out she stayed longer than usual. Before she finally came back to the house she went to the spot where the woodpile had stood, visited the curious little fort which they had built of chopped wood, and then entered the stable. . . . It worried her to know where he would find material for a coffin. She had looked everywhere outside, but had discovered only a few bits of planks and the box in which he had mixed the lime. . . . Hadn't she better remind him of this at once? Then perhaps he could go to the Trönders, east on the Sioux River, and get some lumber from them. . . . Never mind, she wouldn't do anything about it for a few days yet.

. . . If he could only spare her the big chest! . . . Beret fell to looking at it, and grew easier in her mind. . . . That chest had belonged to her great-grandfather, but it must have been in the family long before his day; on it she could make out only the words "*Anno 16—*" . . . the rest was completely worn away. Along the edges and running twice around the middle were heavy iron bands. . . . Beret would go about looking at the chest—would lift the lid and gaze down inside. . . . Plenty of room in there, if they would only put something under her head and back! She felt as if she could sleep safely in that bed.

FROZEN BARN

An abandoned barn and the land it once ruled stand sheathed in ice. Minnetonka-based photographer Bob Firth's images capture the rich details in things most people never look at twice. He collaborated with writer Bill Holm in creating Landscape of Ghosts, *published by Voyageur Press in 1993. The book is a remembrance of things past in rural Minnesota, told through a series of essays and photographs.* (Photograph © Bob Firth/Firth Photo Bank)

Photo by Roleff
Two Harbors, Minn.

Echoes of Cool Red Tunnels

By Jim Klobuchar

For more than three decades, Jim Klobuchar was the journalist and columnist that Minnesotans turned to when they opened their newspaper each and every day.

Klobuchar comes from a long lineage of fine journalists who have roots in Minnesota, including Harrison Salisbury, Eric Sevareid, Gordon Parks, Dave Moore, and Cedric Adams. In the thousands of articles and columns he penned over his forty-three years working for the Minneapolis *StarTribune* and in his fifteen books, Klobuchar proved himself on a daily basis as a writer of uncommon compassion.

Klobuchar was born and raised in Ely on the Iron Range. In between working the mines, he sought to become a writer. From his start in journalism at the Bismarck, North Dakota, newspaper through his years as one of Minnesota's most-read reporters, Klobuchar remained true to his roots, telling the story of everyday "heroes," as he called them—ordinary people who live their lives with a noble courage.

This excerpt from his memoir *Minstrel: My Adventure in Newspapering* (1997) tells of life on the Iron Range and the hopes and dreams of the immigrants who came from afar to work the bountiful Minnesota ore mines.

IN THE HEART OF THE EARTH

Miners pause in their labors in the Fayal underground mine near Eveleth in 1919. Armed with only picks and shovels, they unearthed iron ore by the light of lanterns, helping to earn Minnesota's Iron Range its worldwide reputation as a priceless source for iron in the first decades of the 1900s. This photograph was taken by William Roleff of Two Harbors. (Minnesota Historical Society)

THE CALL OF the wolf won wide popularity among nature lovers as the symbolic sound of northern Minnesota winter in later years. But in the mining town where I grew up, the sound that brought the snow and north wind of approaching winter suddenly close to the skin was the squeal of a dying pig.

Once every late November in my hometown of Ely on the Iron Range, the families gathered at Grandma Rose's to slaughter a pig and make sausage for the winter. It was also Grandpa Joe's, of course, but Rose was the empress of the family and especially of the grandchildren. She gave presents and kisses in profusion. In the family, she combined the highest callings of counselor and chair of the board. You couldn't confuse it with a corporate board. We wouldn't be making blood sausage in her backyard on a November morning if it were that. But there was a roughly constituted round table of family affairs on the Iron Range then. Its moral leadership usually fell to a woman like Rose, whose memory of America reached back to the throngs at Ellis Island, where she could not understand the voices but could understand the surge of excitement she felt and the bewilderment she saw in the faces of the others as they pressed toward the gates of their new land and its deep void of the unknown. That had been nearly a half century before. The country they left, Slovenia in what became Yugoslavia, was a dead end for Rose, for her husband, and for thousands like them. It was dominated by Austria, which, exercising the overlord's prerogative, decided which of the native children could go to school. Sometimes it was as primitive and as cruel as a lineup in the street. Every fifth or tenth child would be selected. The rest had no appeal.

Rose's kids rarely groused about cold rooms in the middle of winter in Minnesota or about rock-headed teachers at school. If she heard it, she listened for a while and then slapped the table. In her broken English, she recalled the scenes of what the immigrants called "the old country." The sound of her hand banging the oak tabletop needed no translation. "Enough," it said.

To her children, she spoke Slovenian most of the time. It was easier all around because they grew up hearing and speaking their parents' tongue, learning the names of the unpronounceable towns where their parents grew up, the Ribnicas and the Crnomelces. The grandchildren didn't bother grappling with the rest of those Slavic syllables. When they bitched, they did it in English, and when they were told off by the family matriarch, it was prompt and in English and didn't allow for rebuttal.

If you were a linguistic expert, you could have unscrambled dialogue like that in the Finnish and Italian homes as well. Add Croatian, Bulgarian, and Greek. I don't know how many made blood sausage on a November morning in the 1930s and 1940s. As children, we assumed it was some kind of ethnic food, unaware that this was common fare among the Scandinavians in town as well as some of the other nationalities. But I don't know how many others gathered the clans on a November Saturday and turned the grinding of sausage into a family festival where wine flowed when the pig was well and truly dead. And Rose brought out a stumpy grinding machine two feet high, and with it a washtub full of boiled pig intestines she used for sausage casings. The sight foreshadowed an axiom I learned years later: if you want to enjoy feasting on hot dogs at a picnic, never tour a sausage factory.

Re-creating the day years later on a drive back to Ely for my grandmother's funeral, I was struck by the tribal quality of that scene of sausage making and reunion on the brink of winter. There couldn't have been much aesthetic content in all of that mess. What I did remember warmly was the sociable sense of ritual that went with a day like that on the Range. Sausage making for the immigrants was a bridge to the old country. The memory of Europe brought them few glints of rekindled joy—the old country with its thin pantries and the boots of the emperor's army and the dead ends. But it was, after all, their homeland and the cradle of their family, and it taught them their songs. So they sang the songs and spoke the language, but the Iron Range was the new frontier of their lives. If they had ever envisioned America as a place where lotus gardens flowered outside their windows and velvet carpets carried them into the streets, they didn't find the gardens and the carpets. Most of them got shantytowns on the edge of the mining pits. The men went into the mines. The women hung the family clothes on the line when the temperature was fifteen degrees below zero. The plumbing, when it came in, was erratic. It wasn't the Austrian government that ruled their lives now, or the czar in Russia, or the kings and queens. Now the mining companies disbursed the money and made most of the rules.

But in the mining town of Minnesota there was one abiding difference from the times and places that had squashed them down before they came to America. Fear had gone out of their lives. So had futility. True, the dirt of the mining town might have been a little deeper than the dirt of the old country. They were embarrassed by their ignorance of the language and having to sequester themselves in their self-protective colonies, where people spoke a language they could understand and nobody laughed at their crudities. But there were schools in this town. Their children would grow up speaking English. If they did their lessons, they could escape the shantytowns and the dark red pits where the immigrant men worked.

On the way to my last visit to my grandmother, driving old Highway 61 from the Twin Cities to the Iron Range, I

"Franklin Mine"
The Franklin open mine was portrayed in oil on canvas by painter Dewey Albinson in 1932 for the Work Projects Administration during the Great Depression. Albinson's blend of realism with cubism gave a sense of the iron ore's use as building blocks for the nation's industry. (Minnesota Historical Society)

prayed for forgiveness and said a prayer of thanks. I came back to my hometown as a newspaper columnist in the midst of a life seasoned with action and familiar with the faces of celebrity. But until that day in December of 1969, I hadn't realized what the mining town on the edge of the wilderness had implanted in my life. I don't think I really comprehended until then the tang and the richness and the wonderful looniness that all of those mixed tongues and cultures had conspired to produce. The names and the insults we threw at each other would probably put us in court in a seventy-five-page defamation suit today. They were thick with derision and mockery, mean and naked. They did eventually take on a softer coat of good-natured ribbing, but that took a while. The nationalities came together, the light-skinned Finns and the darker, maybe faintly menacing

South Slavs and Italians and the rest. Color me a darker, maybe faintly menacing South Slav. The other settlers called the Slovenians and Croatians "garlic gabbers." You can believe that this was one of the politer terms of odium. And when the rest of us heard an unexplained boom from somewhere above the ore tunnels, somebody in Zenith Location (dominated by the Slavs) would smirk with the answer: "The Finnish navy is back in action"—meaning that they were dynamiting fish out on the lake. It didn't matter whether *all* of the Slovenians smelled of garlic or whether there really was a Finnish dynamite flotilla out there on the water. The backbiting gossip and name calling were games, mostly harmless. But they did establish little pieces of turf for the nationalities in town.

The Vermilion Range and its enclaves were isolated from

MINE TRUCK DRIVER
A female truck driver rests against the gigantic wheel of her dump truck at an Iron Range taconite mine in this image by photographer Layne Kennedy. Adept at capturing the essence of people on film, Kennedy's portraits of Minnesotans are colorful, rich, and full of life. (Photograph © Layne Kennedy)

the larger and more prominent Mesabi. Ely was not the Mesabi's Hibbing or Eveleth. Its red riches did not lie in the caverns called open pits, where men could see the sun—or feel the hard clamp of subzero cold—while they and their machines dug those giant concentric circles of the oval mining strip. On the Vermilion Range, where Ely and Tower and Soudan grew, the ore that would become the steel of the automobiles and artillery of America was buried more than a thousand feet beneath the surface. To pry it out of its subterranean lodes, men had to descend into the red tunnels with lamps on their helmets, carrying lunch pails in which their wives or daughters had packed pork chop sandwiches or pasties or Polish sausages, a thermos of coffee, and a chocolate bar or a wedge of homemade pie. In a large elevator suspended beneath a two-inch steel cable, they were lowered into the claustrophobia of a mine shaft sunk a quarter of a mile deep below the mine's head frame. No one ever called it the elevator. It was, simply, "the cage." In the summer between college terms when I worked underground to help pay tuition, I never heard a miner refer to "the cage" with any trace of martyrdom or sarcasm. It was a blunt, unlovely word for a blunt and unlovely vehicle. Nothing much else seemed to fit. Elevators ran in hotels. This was the underground mine. Call it the cage.

Oddly, the cage and the damp tunnels became a gruff forum for the beginnings of mutual tolerance in a laboring town of so many mixed tongues and ethnic feuds transported from the old world. Sensitivity it wasn't. The Range mining towns in those years were outposts of hard-core macho. But if you were an immigrant or a first-generation Finn and your mining partner was a Croatian, the suspicions and the crude jokes tended to dissolve. The bridges were built slowly. They asked about one another's families. They shared the work and the bonus pay that came with harder work. They shared the intramural horseplay and sometimes the fear. Even into the 1940s and 1950s, after much of the mining had been mechanized and federal law had mandated safety practices and the mining companies cooperated, death underground was always a risk. Once or twice a year during the catechism classes of my childhood, I'd look down the aisle of our church and see a black-draped catafalque placed near the altar to bear the coffin of a member of the church killed in a cave-in fourteen hundred feet beneath the surface. It was chilling. It frightened me because my father went underground each day or each night five days a week, round the calendar. Once

he was trapped in a cave-in and buried to his waist. He had been mining since the age of fifteen, when his mother and father died of cancer within a few months of each other, leaving ten children. My father was the oldest. There weren't many foster homes on the Iron Range in the early 1920s. Even if there had been, the creed in the mining town was to keep the family together. There were no trips to the office for aid to the families of dependent children. Nearly twenty years after his death, I still have no idea what my father wrote on the line for "age" in his application to the mining company. There may not have been such a line. If there was, the supervising mining captain ignored it. Here was a kid from the eighth grade trying to support his brothers and sisters, his parents gone. The captain gave him a helmet and a carbide lamp. In the eighth grade he'd received good grades in arithmetic, and in another time he might have been an honor roll student and a college grad. He'd hoped some day to go to sea. It was the one fantasy of his life. He'd read books and listened to sailors, and in his walks to the schoolhouse through the snowdrifts he imagined a career in the United States Navy, visiting the exotic ports of call and breathing the ocean air.

There were no exotic places for a fifteen-year-old swinging a pick a thousand feet below ground. His youngest sister was sheltered in an orphanage in Duluth for a few years, but was restored to the family when the older sisters and the other two brothers were old enough to work. The family survived. The kid who would never see the ocean became a shift boss underground after a few years and married a young woman named Mary, the child of Slovenian immigrants, as he was. Four of his sisters and a brother eventually moved to Milwaukee and married. The two other sisters married and stayed in Ely. So did the two younger brothers. There was no dramatic rise to riches for any of these people, but all lived worthwhile lives. Sympathetic poets might have seen in the underground mine an oblivion of the spirit. No such poetry appeared in our family's archives. The iron mine became the family's salvation. . . . the mine and the teenage boy who would never see the world.

It happened much that way for scores of families in my hometown. It was not enough reason for them to love the underground mine or the mining companies that gave them work. There wasn't much humanitarianism in the relationship of company, miner, and mine. But one of the reasons I gave thanks on the drive to my grandmother's funeral was

> *Sympathetic poets might have seen in the underground mine an oblivion of the spirit. No such poetry appeared in our family's archives. The iron mine became the family's salvation. . . . the mine and the teenage boy who would never see the world.*

DRYING NETS

Commercial fisherman Stanley Sivertson stands surrounded by his drying nets, which he lays out across the floor of an abandoned warehouse when he's not fishing Lake Superior. (Photograph © Layne Kennedy)

seeing the whole sweaty but glorious metaphor of the American idea summarized by the lifetime of this woman who came out of the Slovenian highlands and landed on Ellis Island, scared but thrilled. I remembered her comforting bosom when I was a child. I remembered her sitting beside that funny black meat grinder, churning out dozens of fat and squishy sausages, filling the casings with rice and pork chunks and pig's blood and running a pointed peg through the sausage ends to create a ringlet that would be frozen and kept for the long northern winter.

At that moment she was not a portrait to be confused with Whistler's mother. But she provided, and she made the family unbreakable.

On the Range, and over a wider geography than that, she was an Everywoman of her time, the immigrant matriarch of her family. She and the Finnish and Croatian and Jewish and Polish and Bulgarian and Scandinavian and English and Irish women and the women of a dozen other nationalities

were priceless to the country's future. Their people were disgorged from the steamers by the thousands, expecting no peppermint canes and lemon trees in the new country and without illusions about what lay ahead: leaky roofs and muddy streets in the mining towns, a mole's life in the pits for the men.

They were carried on the corporate books of the time as Cheap Labor. They might not have been aware of that, but it wouldn't have bothered them much if they had been. America was their redemption. It might laugh at their clumsy English and be scared by their foreign faces. But it would pay if they worked. It was huge and unstoppable, America. I didn't know what Grandma Rose's dreams were in the highlands before she left the old country. But in my newspaper column a few days after her funeral, I explored what those dreams might have been and what her reality became. Doing it, I found a different kind of mine on the Iron Range, one not likely to run dry. This one yielded its riches in the thick broth of the mining town's personalities. They carried to Minnesota's north their cacophonous tongues and yearnings, their furies and hilarities. I began bringing the Range into the newspaper. The stories seemed to fascinate our readers, city dwellers and farm people who had always been inquisitive about what lay out there on that strange frontier of ore canyons and people who talked with their hands.

Grandma Rose. I never did decide what she imagined she would find or what she would become. Her husband worked underground for thirty years. His pension amounted to a few bucks a week when he retired. He didn't feel exploited or underpaid. His kids went to school. He had food on the table and pin cherry wine in the basement. In some years it was zinfandel wine, the years when he and a few hundred others contracted with the Casagrandes in Virginia for a load of Michigan grapes. It was legal, more or less, depending on how much wine you made. The cops didn't usually inquire, because the cops had some sizable barrels in their own basements.

Grandma Rose gave me my first Christmas present and a grandmother's last embrace. She saw the country in terms of the bread and the integrity it gave her family, in the beans and the dandelion salad they ate in the early years and something better as they grew older and the unions got stronger and the wages went up. . . .

On the Range, the tenderness and guidance came from the mother. The father set the rules. When necessary, he gave the whacks. This was not exactly gender equality, nor did that form of family discipline pay much attention to the Beatitudes. In fact, it would horrify family counselors today, and conceivably get the old man tossed in jail. It's simply the way it was, the last stand of the patriarchal fiefdom brought over from old Europe. Neither my brother nor I got many whacks from our father, or many embraces. Mike never felt comfortable revealing affection. He was the father in the style of his own father, who acquired the style in the hills of Slovenia, where the idea went back a few millennia. The stoical, distant father was hardly peculiar to the Iron Range. Not many social attitudes have clung so obstinately in humanity's stumbling attempts over the centuries to arrange its roles and privileges. It took the revolutions of the 1960s and the new-age psy-

chology plus the courts and a million television sitcoms to produce some symptoms of democracy in the house. What might have been different on the Iron Range was the harshness of the work, which heightened the husband and father's role as the Provider. . . .

Was there a place for genuine love in this house?

Yes, there was. Love may have been defined differently in a home like ours in a mining town in the 1930s and 1940s, in marriages like that of my mother and father. In today's relationships and families, love is intimacy and awareness of each other's feelings; it is respecting differences, sharing and forgiving.

Most of those qualities were present in our house and the houses of our neighbors, but not as candidly and self-consciously as we know them today. It was not written then that love means showing affection in spontaneous ways, although every now and then I'd see outbursts at a family gathering and I remember enjoying the sight. In our house, the love that my mother and father expressed for each other and for their children began with the sanctity of the marriage. Most people in my town and in most of the towns of America in those years believed that the marriage vow meant what it said: for better or for worse. Until death do us part. One man, one woman, one marriage, one family. That was their commitment. It meant acceptance of the other—which did not have to be the same as docility—as long as that acceptance

COMMERCIAL FISHERMAN
Commercial fisherman Dick Eckel docks out of Hovlund, casting his nets into the Lake Superior waters and hauling in his catch by hand. Eckel is one of the last handful of Great Lakes commercial fishermen. (Photograph © Layne Kennedy)

did not condone lifelong brutality. It meant loyalty and it meant dividing the burden. It meant my mother praying at midnight when my father was late getting home from work; she was afraid there'd been a cave-in. The only time I ever saw my father cry was when I was ten, and my mother went to the hospital for an examination that both were afraid would reveal cancer, but didn't. My brother said the one time he saw Mike in tears was while he was writing an accident report at home the day after a timber collapse killed one of his crew members in the tunnel where they worked.

Marriage counselors of today might look at that stoical nuclear family of the mining town with a certain amount of commitment, they would argue, should lock the partners into lifelong misery or the demeaning of one of them. Who would argue with that principle today? But where I lived, I saw no prolonged misery resulting from the marriage-for-keeps, nor many dysfunctional children who emerged from it. . . .

While the Range politics of the midcentury were freewheeling and the beer joints were boisterous, the churches were oases of order and stability.

The normal rules of the market never impressed the Range mentality very much, because one way to make it through the bad times was to build communal networks—not much different from the circle-the-wagons strategies of the prairie in the 1870s. The house in which I grew up was towed eighteen miles from the then-abandoned taconite settlement in Babbitt in 1935. The house cost my mother and father one hundred dollars. They got the tow free in exchange for some deer meat my father had shared with the trucker the year before. Babbitt died in the 1920s (to be reincarnated years later) because the engineers lacked a practical system for extracting iron particles from the hard rock. Eventually a process of magnetic separation was perfected. It saved every town on the Iron Range from the ghosts after the ore ran out in the pits. But a dozen houses came onto the market in Babbitt in the 1920s and 1930s. The small wood frame house my father and the trucker dragged eighteen miles more than sixty years ago is still standing. My mother, now ninety, has kept it immaculate. The steel rail my father found on a deserted track is still there as the support for the living room ceiling, hidden by the stuccoed arch he built under it. The house had to be torn down on its arrival from Babbitt; a basement was poured, and the house was rebuilt. The basement was done in eight hours on a summer Sunday. It cost my parents a dozen ham sandwiches and two cases of beer. Practically nobody hired contractors to build a house on the Range in the 1930s. The biggest resources in town always were the rela-

tives.

Sometime before the men went underground to work, or when they got there, they became amateur plumbers, electricians, carpenters, and masons. On the appointed Sunday morning, my uncles showed up with wheelbarrows, trowels, hammers, carpenter's levels, and large appetites. Most of them went to Father Mike's 6:00 a.m. service at St. Anthony's Church, the one he gave in the Slovenian language. If they were going to pour the basement they had to show up at St. Anthony's before dawn or risk hellfire until next Sunday. That was the unequivocal proposition the Reverend Frank J. Mihelcic put to his flock. Father Mike was born in the Yugoslavian province of Herzegovina. His mission of saving souls in our town was enhanced by his deftness with the Slovenian language, which most of the church veterans spoke. But he was handicapped by the fact that most of the undergrounders did not pursue salvation very zealously. Father Mike ignored these discouragements. He was a heavyset guy with a red, fleshy face and a pug nose that spread comfortably from cheek to cheek. He was hardly the only clergyman in town. The Lutherans and Methodists and Presbyterians all had spiritual shelter. There was even a period when the Holy Rollers established a foothold in Ely. The Iron Range was that kind of outland. Communists rang doorbells in the middle of the Depression, candidly recruiting. On the Mesabi Range, they even found a candidate who got elected to Congress for one term wearing a hammer and sickle in his lapel. The attempt to socialize the Range didn't last long. The mining companies represented a powerful, offstage political force because of the influence they exerted on school financing and, of course, on jobs. They conducted their own kind of jungle war against radical politics and eventually so did the unions.

While the Range politics of the midcentury were freewheeling and the beer joints were boisterous, the churches were oases of order and stability. But the call process in the Protestant churches meant that their pastors came and went. Frank J. Mihelcic stayed with the obstinacy of the Rock of Ages. This was his home, the impregnable seal of his stewardship. It was also his barony. He ran the church and terrorized some of the politicians. He rarely agonized over the doctrine of separation of church and state. If a priest was going to be a power broker as well as an apostle of redemption on the Iron Range, he didn't bury himself in the parsonage. He went into the street and a few times into the bars. He did it out of generosity of spirit and a lively interest in keeping the pews filled on Sunday mornings. More than one stoned parishioner found himself being lifted out of a snowbank on Saturday night by the ham hands of Frank Mihelcic, making one of his periodic winter rounds. The reverend usually had the chivalry to leave his shaky ward at the gate after walking him home, assuming the parishioner had regained his bearings well enough to find his way to the front door.

Frank Mihelcic's roaring pulpit style camouflaged a pastoral gentleness and compassion that often startled his parishioners when they came to him with personal grief. At those hours he was friend and consoler. But nobody messed with him when he got into the full flight of one of his Sunday-morning condemnations of the collection-plate slackers. The consuming vow of his life was to build a new church, high on the hill where the parish house stood, overlooking Shagawa Lake. He created a budget and a timetable. When they faltered, there were no urgent congregational meetings. Father Mike stood behind the altar and thundered his indictments. He invoked God, St. Michael, the souls of the deceased, and the evidence from his Saturday-night patrols. He threatened damnation and promised to take no prisoners the next time the laggards showed up in the confession box.

When all four of the underground mines were working full shifts—especially during the war, when they unearthed millions of tons for the defense factories, round the clock—the town supported more than five thousand people.

"You spend twenty dough-lar in the bars," he shouted, "but you don't have a dime for choorch." Scores of nervous hands could then be seen sliding into pockets.

On the day the new church was formally opened and dedicated, he opened the books.

There was no mortgage.

The new church was free and clear the day it opened. Father Mike could have committed himself to the saints and died fulfilled right there. He didn't. The next Sunday he was roasting some female tourists for desecrating the church by showing up in flimsy clothes. He's gone now, but there's hardly a doubt that Frank Mihelcic is flourishing with the saints. One exposure to his Sunday sermons and the devil would have run up the flag on the spot.

Father Mike and his autocracy aside, the real political leverage in town came from the usual Iron Range powerhouses: the mining companies, the merchants, and later the unions and the Democratic-Farmer-Labor Party. One way or another their interests merged in times of stress. And when those interests combined with the legitimate strivings of the mixed nationalities, an earthy kind of democracy began to settle over the Range before World War II, replacing the old enmities. Common problems outweighed conflicts and

suspicions. Recognizing one another's strengths and struggles came slowly among the ethnic clans. Each had its own acreage. The Finns staked out the heights near the big lake, Shagawa, early in the immigration, and inevitably the place became known as Finn Hill. Woodland lovers who could afford it moved to the highland in the pines on the south edge of town up the Moose Lake road. There was space for spreading out. In fact, there was need for it. This was no hamlet sitting above the ore veins. When all four of the underground mines were working full shifts—especially during the war, when they unearthed millions of tons for the defense factories, round the clock—the town supported more than five thousand people.

The Slavs congregated in more communal quarters, which in the early immigration had the look of dingy Balkan ghettos transported to the mining frontier. But they worked their way out of them and built or bought their own homes with money they saved or borrowed from the bank. The banks eventually learned the wisdom of liberal loan policies. The immigrants had come to work and to stay. Most of their children lived by the same dogma. Almost nobody defaulted on a loan. Intermarriage between the ethnic clans gradually changed the town's social attitudes and made most of the prejudices obsolete, sped by the amorous hotbloods of the first and second generations who weren't much impressed by old-country feuds. So mutual esteem, while it often came grudgingly, came. It came in the tardy respect conferred on the Jewish merchants in Ely, the Gordons and the Rosenblooms. No point is served by dredging up the derogatory names they were called privately by some of the townspeople. The words were bad then and they're even worse today.

Mike Gordon and Phillip Rosenbloom were the proprietors of two of the clothing stores in town. They sold their clothes off simple racks, usually for a few bucks less than what their competitors were charging in the metropolis of Virginia, the Queen City of the Arrowhead, fifty miles down the highway. They were reserved and courteous to their customers but didn't feel comfortable addressing most of them by their first names, so when the lady of the house came in, it was usually, "Good afternoon, missus. How are you?"

Money for extra indoor clothes began running out in the middle 1930s. But if you walked to work in a northern Minnesota winter, or hung out the Monday-morning wash with bare fingers in twenty-below weather, you needed clothes.

No one carried plastic cards in their wallets or purses.

Credit was extended if you didn't have enough cash. But something more than bookkeeping credit was needed to keep hundreds of families afloat on the Range during the Depression. Open pits shut down for months at a time on the Mesabi. In Ely, where winter offered no impediment to drilling for ore in the underground mines and therefore no excuse for closing them, the shafts stayed open, but the work hours were cut back. Miners would walk to the government employment offices and apply for a few days "for the city," or "for the county." They shoveled snow, drove trucks or cut the tall grass in the roadbeds with scythes. But eventually they would have to walk into a clothing store for a heavier coat or boots.

"I'm a little short this week," they might say.

"It's OK," the Gordons or the Rosenblooms would say.

"I might be a little short next week, too."

"It's OK."

"I don't know about next month."

At this point in the dialogue, as my relatives explained it, the proprietor would begin to smile with a mixture of hope and resignation.

"You are a customer here eight, nine years?"

"Right."

"You always pay?"

"Yes."

"Well, you pay when you can pay. I wait. Anytime is OK. Maybe you need some wool socks."

The democracy might have been too young and shallow to assimilate the Gordons and the Rosenblooms into the rough and tumble of a mining society that carried the old world prejudices to America. And here those prejudices were quickly layered into the new world prejudices. No all-nations love feast erupted among the immigrants on the Range until decades later, when festivals actually broke out with bands, picnics, and hundreds of people dancing under stars by a lakeshore. Chicago, Pittsburgh, Cleveland, Gary, Indiana, and dozens of other ethnic magnets would give the same testimony about the early years. And maybe the Gordons and the Rosenblooms were a little wary about what they might find out if they got too chummy with their customers. But hundreds in my hometown who lived through the Depression could not—and would not want to—deny the humanity they heard in the simple words from the Jewish merchant: "It's OK. I wait."

The Gordons and the Rosenblooms were hardly alone among the merchants who offered generous credit in those years. In my hometown the Lozars and Makis and Kovaches

DULUTH

A ship approaches the Duluth lift bridge on its way into the port city's famous harbor. (Photograph © Layne Kennedy)

and Kangases and Zupanciches did it. Their sympathies were real, but so were their views of the world. There wasn't much choice. The government didn't give food stamps. The only welfare service available was called, in a gem of New Deal euphemism, "Relief." Most people avoided the Relief office. It seemed to be an admission of something unclean. Charity.

As though there is something unclean about charity.

But that was pride and stubbornness, which is why the merchant would say, "It's OK." Yet it wasn't a one-way street. Almost everybody worked a family vegetable garden or kept chickens, sometimes pigs. This was not then the north woods of nature-smitten dreamers. Roosters were more valuable than canoes. It was not uncommon to see a woman walking into a grocery store with bags of lettuce or eggs. The barter system was reborn. The Middle Ages weren't that far behind.

Yet I can't honestly recall any true horror stories about the hardship inflicted on the people in my hometown during that national trauma. The mines cut back, but they put food on the shelves. What the mines didn't provide for the table, the green grass did. Dandelion salad never went out of style. There were millions of dandelion plants to be picked, and on any given day in summer the grandmothers were out in their babushkas with their water pails, gathering dandelions until they overflowed the pails. Dandelion salad probably wouldn't get top billing today as the piece de resistance at your average five-star restaurant, but the women figured out a way to give it a verve that raised it above the level of chewable grass. Beans, vinegar and oil, and warm bacon chunks spruced it up. Hot bread from the oven rescued almost any meal from mediocrity. Corn mush in milk (or coffee) at breakfast ushered hundred of kids on the Iron Range to school. So did grilled blood sausage with its stomach-sinking freight of hot rice and pork chunks.

Which meant that while it didn't take much encouragement to eat breakfast on the Range, it did take some character. At night the queen of desserts was blueberry pie, invariably made from blueberries picked by the whole family the previous summer, when we had advanced through the moss swamps with lard cans boiled clean and outfitted with handles. Blueberry picking was the Sunday recreation of choice. The goal was to fill a wooden box the size of a beer case. The box had served earlier as a dynamite crate underground, where it was called a powder box. We usually picked from midmorning to nightfall. The family down the block had to break it off one Sunday when a black bear muscled into their patch.

Yet the ethnic colonies produced genuine gourmet cooking, given half the chance and enough uncluttered space in the living room. It took maneuvering to make *potica* in Slavic homes. Pronounce it *poh-teet-sah*, but don't eat it if you're battling the scale. *Potica* in its pure, Balkan incarnation was and is a dark walnut bread rolled in thin layers and sliced like jelly roll. It harmonizes naturally with baked ham and, when it appeared in a miner's lunch pail in the underground eating shacks, it was always a sign that he had managed once more to achieve good terms with his wife. The *potica* most of us coveted, however, was actually a Balkanization of the Austro-German strudel, a suicidally rich pastry rolled in layers of dough as fragile as tissue paper and filled with nuts and apple butter. The rolling of enough dough to fill three or four cookie pans with coiled strudel required engineering skills. With faces caked in flour dust, the women usually rolled it on the large wooden ovals of their living room tables and draped it over the edges in translucent curtains that flirted with the rug. In that condition it not only held the promise of a rare weekend of feasting but also provided excellent cover for kids playing hide and seek.

The Finns concocted a fish soup that won plaudits from visiting chefs who came up from Chicago to fish on Basswood Lake. The Italians hoarded their recipes for porketta. And everybody made pasties and claimed to be the originators. Pasties—pronounced with a short *a*—are meat and vegetables pies. There are still a dozen places where you can buy them on the Range. A few diehard cafes and grocery stores in the Twin Cities whose proprietors are expatriates from the Range also try to nourish the ebbing memories. Pasties were the housewives' salvation when the refrigerator shelves started to empty. The women could always grab a bowlful of potatoes, chop some meat, throw in a few rutabaga slices and sprigs of parsley, roll some dough, and extract a half dozen pasties from the oven in a few minutes. If you ate one at a sitting, you were full. If you ate two, you were heroic. The Finns loudly claimed to have exported pasties from Upper Michigan mining towns to Minnesota. My mother always disputed that, believing pasties were native to Ribnica, where her mother was born in the woodcarving country of Slovenia. The Swedes and Norwegians usually stayed out of it; they were outnumbered on the Range and at supper time generally sought refuge around their walleyes and boiled potatoes. It took them years to figure out that when the southern Europeans yelled and screamed at each other about food, love, or heaven, it didn't mean they were mad. It was their natural speaking volume, a rolling din.

SNOWED IN
Snow sheathes mailboxes along the Gunflint Trail. (Photograph © Richard Hamilton Smith)

Cruising God's Country

By Sigurd F. Olson

Sigurd Olson was a modern-day voyageur, born centuries after the first voyageurs paddled the waters of northern Minnesota. His books also marked him as a modern-day transcendentalist in the fashion of Henry David Thoreau, sharing through his writing his conviction that the solitude of nature was a basic need of all human beings.

Olson was born in Chicago in 1900, but raised primarily in northern Wisconsin. Following service in World War I, he received a B.S. degree from the University of Wisconsin. In 1920, he settled in Ely, where he would largely live the rest of his life, teaching at Ely Junior College and writing about the great wilderness that is the Boundary Waters.

Olson's first book, *The Singing Wilderness* (1956), sang the praises of nature. It was followed by numerous other books and collections of essays and articles, including *Listening Point* (1958), *The Lonely Land* (1961), *Runes of the North* (1963), *Open Horizons* (1969), and others. Olson's writing—and his life—was devoted to understanding, explaining, and protecting the wilderness for future generations.

This article was Olson's first published piece, appearing in the Milwaukee *Journal* in 1921 and launching *The Collected Works of Sigurd F. Olson: The Early Writings: 1921–1934*, published by Voyageur Press in 1988. Already in this premier essay the bud of all of Olson's subsequent writing and philosophy can be seen, ready to blossom.

GRAY WOLF

Photographer Jim Brandenburg's name has been linked to his images of wolves. He began wielding a camera as a photojournalist for the Worthington Daily Globe *before moving on to* National Geographic *magazine. His most famous book,* White Wolf: Living with an Arctic Legend *(1988), was the result of his work alongside noted University of Minnesota wolf researcher L. David Mech on Ellesmere Island. Since then, Brandenburg has published numerous other books focused on wolves as well as other aspects of America's surviving wilderness.* (Photograph © Jim Brandenburg/Minden Pictures)

WHEN THE GREAT Creator had almost finished this wonderful country he stopped in his labors and pondered. There was one thing lacking, a spot more beautiful than all the rest where his children could come and soothe their weary spirits. A sanctuary, far from the smoke of cities and the discordant clamor of industry, a wilderness unsullied by the hand of man. God saw all that was to happen. He saw the ravaging of his forests, the despoiling of his streams and lakes by the greedy, unthinking hands of those who would know no beauty and see only in the wonders of nature, resources for filling their own already bursting coffers.

He also knew that some of his children would love nature and its beauties as they should. That the trees would be their temples and the glories of mountain and forest their religion. He knew that they would weep at the wanton destruction of the nature that would mean to them life itself. So for these who would deeply love and truly understand nature in all its moods, He set aside a little bit of Paradise, inaccessible for those who would despoil it.

East of the Rainy Lake country and north of the rugged shores of Lake Superior lies a virgin wilderness almost too beautiful to describe. It would be as easy to paint a perfect sunset or the northern lights as to do the country justice.

It is a primitive wilderness of lakes, streams and mountains where the only sounds are the laughing of the loons, the slap of the beaver's tail and the sloshing around of moose and deer in the bays. It is today as it was before Columbus discovered this country, untouched, untarnished. The winds still whisper through the virgin timber, the waves on Big Saganaga still lap hungrily at the rocky shore. The cry of the great northern loon echoes and re-echoes from Lake Superior to Hudson Bay. The moose and deer come down to drink still unafraid, down trails deeply worn through centuries of use. The beaver build their dams and the crash of the falling popple and ash is unheard by human ears. The wilderness is teeming with life. Everything is yet as God left it; perfect. He had planned well.

Let us cruise for a while, just you and I, through this wonderland that was set aside for us.

We have passed through many lakes, made countless portages and now at last are in the heart of the wilderness. Our camp is on a rocky island covered with balsam and spruce. The canoe is pulled up high and dry. I am busy with the fire. You perhaps have just finished cutting balsam boughs for our beds, and being a little tired after the long day of paddling against the wind, you light your pipe and wander down to the shore. A fallen spruce offers a good resting place so you sit down and look out over the lake.

All is still, the water is smooth as glass except when disturbed by the jumping of lake trout. The heavily timbered shores are reflected as from a mirror in the waters and as you gaze you sometimes catch yourself wondering which is which, the reflection or the shore. A white throated sparrow calls so far away and sweetly, you can hardly believe a note could be so clear and faint and still be heard. You stand there in awe, the silence almost overcomes you, and a queer feeling comes to your throat. God! how beautiful it all is, and your soul unconsciously goes out in gratitude to the creator who has saved this little bit of heaven for you.

Suddenly you are startled. A weird screaming peal of maniacal laughter rends the silence like a knife. Not only once, but peal upon peal, each more exultant than the first. A cold shiver travels up and down your spine. You wish you could kill that thing that spoiled it all. But it is only the call of the loon and it is answered far off to the north. You can't help but wonder how far that call will travel, perhaps way up to the Hudson Bay, who knows.

ABOVE: "NEWS FROM HOME"
N. C. Wyeth's 1915 oil painting of voyageurs reading letters from their far-distant homes captures the feel for the days of the fur trade that plied its way through the rivers and lakes of Sigurd Olson's beloved northwoods. (Minnesota Historical Society)

OPPOSITE PAGE: CAMPING LEGS
The mosquito bites, bandaged knees, and Swiss Army knife hanging on its leather lanyard read like a resumé of a seasoned veteran of the Boundary Waters Canoe Area. (Photograph © Layne Kennedy)

As the echoes come back again and again from nameless lakes far away and finally cease, the silence is deeper than ever for everything has a place in God's plan, even the laughing of the loon.

It is almost dark. The sun has set, leaving the west a lurid tumbled mass of burnished gold. The sunset seems almost fierce in its intensity, not peaceful and glowing but instead a sullen angry red. The tent gleams ghostly in the shadow of a huge spruce. I have been cooking supper and the odor of bacon and coffee assails your nostrils and you remember that you are still alive and ravenously hungry after the long day of paddling and portaging.

After supper, our pipes. The smoke curls up and its fragrance adds the final touch to a day that has been lived, not existed. We take out our map and by the light of the campfire find we are on an island on Ottertrack Lake. It is the most beautiful we have struck so far and if it were not for the restless call of that "Something lost behind the Ranges," we would camp here, but like Kipling's explorer we decide that upon the morrow we will look beyond to see what awaits us there.

We are sitting smoking in front of the tent. The smoke from our dying campfire curls lazily upward. It is dark now but over toward the east the tops of the spruces are faintly illumined. We watch expectantly up the water way. First, a thin rim of silver, then slowly, majestically, golden mellow, a glorious summer moon rises dripping out of the dark placid waters of Ottertrack. The spruces are sharply silhouetted for a moment and then the wilderness is bathed in mellow moonlight. Even the sharp old stub over on the shore has something soft and beautiful about it. We sit in silence drinking in the radiant glory about us. Words would be sacrilege. The mournful long drawn wail of a timber wolf comes down from the north and you can't help but shiver a little. A silvery waterway leads directly to our little island. Now it is smooth and polished and now strewn with a million diamonds as a riffle of wind roughens the surface. Peacefulness and contentment is our lot.

Though we are poor in worldly goods, can anyone else love the forests, lakes and streams any more than we do? Our bodies are still strong and full of the vigor of life. We look forward to years of happiness, for life is good to those who know how to live. We do not ever hope to accumulate vast worldly wealth but shall gather instead something far more valuable, a store of memories. When we reach the twilight of

SUNSET ON RAINY LAKE
The sun sets over a lone island on Rainy Lake in the Voyageurs National Park. (Photograph © Layne Kennedy)

LONE TREE
A lone tree stands as a sentinel above a small isle on Lake Three in the Boundary Waters Canoe Area. (Photograph © Gary Alan Nelson)

life we can look back and say, "We are glad we lived as we did." Life has been good to us. We will not be afraid of death, because we will have drunk to the full the cup of happiness and contentment that only close communion with nature can give.

Our pipes are out and the moon is rising high in the heavens. We turn in for the night and sleep as only men can in beds of balsam in the wilderness.

Awake at dawn, for dawn is the best part of the day in the wilderness. The trees and brush are dripping with dew. The birds are bursting their little throats with warbling melody. Everything is fresh and clean. A dip in the icy clear waters of the lake and our toilet is complete. The sun is just coming up over in the bay toward the east. The faint white, low, hanging mist quickly disappears before its warming rays. A bull moose that we hadn't seen before is revealed standing up to his knees in the water of a bay five hundred yards up shore. He hasn't seen us and is busy eating lily pad roots. We watch expectantly as ducking his head and neck under water he comes up in a shower of spray, a bunch of lily roots dripping in his mouth. The sunlight glints on his widely spreading horns as he stands transfixed and looks in our direction. He watches us a little while and then leisurely steps out of the water. We can hear the brush crack as he works his way up over the rise. We get one last glimpse of him as he stands on top of the ridge and looks down upon us.

The trout are jumping and a pair of loons are laughing and splashing water with their wings. The water is so clear that we can see the fish feeding along the shore.

After breakfast we break camp, dip our paddles and are off for new country and new adventures. We paddle close to shore as there is always more of interest there than anywhere else. A mallard hen flies out in front of the canoe, quacking and making believe she is crippled. We soon see the cause of her discomfiture. A flock of little brown chicks are skittering for the shore as fast as their little legs and wings will take them. They hide in all sorts of nooks and peep out timidly at us thinking they are hidden. We glide along through lake after lake, sometimes making portages from one lake to another. Some of the portages are steep and rocky so a man with a pack and a canoe has all he can do to keep his footing. In some places beaver dams have to be crossed and marshy places waded

through, not wet enough to float a canoe but too wet to walk upon. The beaver are very active and evidences of their logging operations are to be seen everywhere. They are so tame that we see them swimming about in broad daylight. When we get too close, down they go with a mighty flap of their tails. We are paddling easily along when the sound of a waterfall reaches our ears.

Paddling in toward shore we leave the canoe and follow up the sound. It must be small because we hear only a faint trickling over the rock. After a hundred yards or so we come to a steep face of rock nearly perpendicular and perhaps one hundred feet in height. A spring fed brook breaks over the top and spreads over the face of the rock like a thin transparent veil. The sun breaking through the birches seems to touch the veil with silver light so we call it the "Crystal Sheen." The little fall is in a grove of slender white birches. The ground and the rock itself is carpeted with the most delicately tinted green moss. Everything is so exquisitely beautiful that one can't help but wonder if this isn't really a part of fairyland. A troupe of tiny fairies with gauzelike wings bathing in the spray of the falls would have made the picture perfect.

Leaving reluctantly we resume our paddling. The steady swish, swish of our paddles soon carries us many miles northward. It's a pleasure to watch your paddle in the clear water, and the little ever present whirlpool that you make with every stroke. We go through a narrow neck and presently the water becomes swifter. We are in a river and before we know it are racing along very swiftly. White water breaking over jagged rocks warns us to keep our distance. A sharp rock

SILENT WINGS
A great gray owl swoops in on silent wings to strike its prey. (Photograph © Bill Marchel)

almost seems to leap at us out of the foam but a quick swerve of the paddle and we slip past. Now we are bounding and shooting through spray and white water. It takes quick thinking, and quicker acting to keep away from the rocks now. The trees on shore seem to shoot past and the rocks are getting thicker. A patch of white water shows up ahead. You try your best to head the canoe to one side. Now we are in it. The sickening sound of a rock grating on the bottom of the canoe and we stop in mid stream. We paddle desperately, the canoe starts to swing. Two more feet and we are done for. A last desperate stroke and we slip off into the current. The water soon becomes quieter and we find ourselves cruising smoothly along through another lake, ever northward. This lake is dotted with rocky islands covered with spruce and Norway pine. Gulls are flying around screaming and flying low over our heads. Evidently this must be their nesting ground.

We are both tired so head the canoe for a pretty little island near the center of the lake. It is a good camping place and the weird beauty of the lake with its many rocky islands and screaming gulls appeals to us so we decide to stop for the night. The rock is covered with heavy lichen which makes a fine bed. The tent is soon up and supper on the way. After supper, our pipes alight, we lay on our backs and gaze up at the lazily drifting clouds. One more day had been added to our stock of memories.

And so we travel through hundreds of lakes and rivers, drink in the beauties of countless water falls, rapids and virgin forests, see naked grandeur as God intended it to be, unscathed by the hand of man. When we end up our cruise and our canoes grate on a sandy beach for the last time, our hearts are heavy and yet how happy. We were ragged and unkempt but what mattered was that our hearts were filled to over-flowing. We came back empty handed but oh, how rich we were. We could say with Kipling's explorer on his return, "Have I named one single river? Have I claimed one single acre? Have I kept one single nugget? No not I. Because my price was paid me ten times over by my maker. But you wouldn't understand it. You go up and occupy."

ABOVE: **CANOE BUILDER**
Old-time birchbark canoe maker Bill Hafeman of Big Fork rests for a spell amid a collection of his wares. (Photograph © Layne Kennedy)

OPPOSITE PAGE: **SUNRISE**
The first rays of the rising sun are reflected in the waters and rocks of Lake Superior at Tettegouche State Park. (Photograph © Gary Alan Nelson)

"Earth-Diver"

 As the sun rises through the morning mist, a common loon surfaces from a dive in the midst of a lake and shakes the water from its wings. Creation stories from around the world tell of the loon as the "Earth-Diver." In these stories, the loon dives to the depths of a flooded world and brings back a bit of earth in its beak to create the first land. An Anishinaabe legend holds that the first act in the creation of the world was the voice of the Spirit-Creator calling across the void to become embodied in the cry of the loon. As the Sun then rose out of the darkness, the first light distinguished itself from the darkness and became embodied in the black and white plumage of the loon. (Photograph © Richard Hamilton Smith)

CHAPTER THREE

MAIN STREET

"Everybody prays in a different way."
—Brenda Ueland, *Strength to Your Sword Arm*, 1993

Main Street was made both famous and infamous in *Main Street*, Sinclair Lewis's masterpiece novel of small-town satire. Minnesota has long been a state proud of its satirists poking gentle and barbed humor at our own ways, a writing style that may be an extension—good or bad—of coffeeshop gab and gossip. These stories and excerpts display masters of the craft, offering a window back to our past and a mirror to ourselves.

ABOVE: **"DISCUSSION"**
Winthrop artist Bennet Swanson's oil painting captures the gab and gossip shared at a small-town café. Swanson painted the image in the 1930s under the auspices of the Work Projects Administration. (Minnesota Historical Society)

OPPOSITE: **WORLD'S LARGEST BALL OF TWINE**
Francis A. Johnson of Darwin amassed the world's largest ball of twine over a lifetime of collecting bits and pieces of baler twine. The massive ball weighs a whopping 21,140 pounds and measures twelve feet in circumference. Hanging onto the "world's largest" record has not been easy, however. Inspired by Johnson's masterpiece, a pretender to the throne, Frank Stoeber of Cawker City, Kansas, began collecting his own twine ball, tying together 1.6 million feet of baler twine into a ball eleven feet in circumference. Stoeber died just when the record seemed within his grasp, and Johnson retained the crown. Both balls of twine are on display to this day as fitting tributes to their creators' earthly labors. (Photograph © Wayne Gudmundson)

The Busy Body and the Good Influence

By Sinclair Lewis

Harry Sinclair Lewis was the king of Minnesotan satirists. With his masterpiece, *Main Street* (1920), Lewis launched a style of Minnesota satire that has become one of the state's great art forms, stretching from Lewis to F. Scott Fitzgerald, Garrison Keillor, and filmmakers Ethan and Joel Coen's movie *Fargo*.

Lewis was born in 1885 in Sauk Centre, the town that became the model for Gopher Prairie of *Main Street*. With his bestselling book, he sullied the myth of the small town as God's country, exposing the narrow-mindedness and smug complacency that he witnessed in his hometown.

Lewis continued to spear small towns and their inhabitants in his other well-known novels, *Babbitt* (1922), *Arrowsmith* (1925), *Elmer Gantry* (1927), and *Dodsworth* (1929). In 1930, he became the first American author to win the Nobel Prize for Literature, but it was only in later years that Sauk Centre was willing to forgive its native son.

These two excerpts from *Main Street* portray the town's Busy Body and Good Influence, and are prime examples of Lewis's pointed wit. The duo come to call on newlywed Carol Kennicott, who has just moved to town from the big city, bringing her luggage of lofty ideals, hoity-toity concepts, and dreams of introducing art, literature, culture, and social reforms to Gopher Prairie— items that the town can definitely do without.

"HAIL! HAIL! THE DAIRY PRINCESS!"
Minneapolis artist Faye Passow's 1995 vision of the Minnesota dairy princess is crowned by a tiara of Swiss cheese.

Despite Vida Sherwin's lively blue eyes, if you had looked at her in detail you would have found her face slightly lined, and not so much sallow as with the bloom rubbed off; you would have found her chest flat, and her fingers rough from needle and chalk and penholder; her blouses and plain cloth skirts undistinguished; and her hat worn too far back, betraying a dry forehead. But you never did look at Vida Sherwin in detail. You couldn't. Her electric activity veiled her. She was as energetic as a chipmunk. Her fingers fluttered; her sympathy came out in spurts; she sat on the edge of a chair in eagerness to be near her auditor, to send her enthusiasms and optimism across.

She rushed into the room pouring out: "I'm afraid you'll think the teachers have been shabby in not coming near you, but we wanted to give you a chance to get settled. I am Vida Sherwin, and I try to teach French and English and a few other things in the high school."

"I've been hoping to know the teachers. You see, I was a librarian——"

"Oh, you needn't tell me. I know all about you! Awful how much I know—this gossipy village. We need you so much here. It's a dear loyal town (and isn't loyalty the finest thing in the world!) but it's a rough diamond, and we need you for the polishing, and we're ever so humble——" She stopped for breath and finished her compliment with a smile.

"If I *could* help you in any way—— Would I be committing the unpardonable sin if I whispered that I think Gopher Prairie is a tiny bit ugly?"

"Of course it's ugly. Dreadfully! Though I'm probably the only person in town to whom you could safely say that. (Except perhaps Guy Pollock the lawyer—have you met him?—oh, you *must*!—he's simply a darling—intelligence and culture and so gentle.) But I don't care so much about the ugliness. That will change. It's the spirit that gives me hope. It's sound. Wholesome. But afraid. It needs live creatures like you to awaken it. I shall slave-drive you!"

"Splendid. What shall I do? I've been wondering if it would be possible to have a good architect come here to lecture."

"Ye-es, but don't you think it would be better to work with existing agencies? Perhaps it will sound slow to you, but I was thinking—— It would be lovely if we could get you to teach Sunday School."

Carol had the empty expression of one who finds that she has been affectionately bowing to a complete stranger. "Oh yes. But I'm afraid I wouldn't be much good at that. My religion is so foggy."

"I know. So is mine. I don't care a bit for dogma. Though I do stick firmly to the belief in the fatherhood of God and the brotherhood of man and the leadership of Jesus. As you do, of course."

Carol looked respectable and thought about having tea.

"And that's all you need teach in Sunday School. It's the personal influence. Then there's the library-board. You'd be so useful on that. And of course there's our women's study club—the Thanatopsis Club."

"Are they doing anything? Or do they read papers made out of the Encyclopedia?"

Miss Sherwin shrugged. "Perhaps. But still, they are so earnest. They will respond to your fresher interest. And the Thanatopsis does do a good social work—they've made the city plant ever so many trees, and they run the rest-room for farmers' wives. And they do take such an interest in refinement and culture. So—in fact, so very unique."

Carol was disappointed—by nothing very tangible. She said politely, "I'll think them all over. I must have a while to look around first."

Miss Sherwin darted to her, smoothed her hair, peered at her. "Oh, my dear, don't you suppose I know? These first tender days of marriage—they're sacred to me. Home, and children that need you, and depend on you to keep them alive, and turn to you with their wrinkly little smiles. And the hearth and——" She hid her face from Carol as she made an activity of patting the cushion of her chair, but she went on with her former briskness:

"I mean, you must help us when you're ready. . . . I'm afraid you'll think I'm conservative. I am! So much to conserve. All this treasure of American ideals. Sturdiness and democracy and opportunity. Maybe not at Palm Beach. But, thank heaven, we're free from such social distinctions in Gopher Prairie. I have only one good quality—overwhelming belief in the brains and hearts of our nation, our state, our town. It's so strong that sometimes I do have a tiny effect on the haughty ten-thousandaires. I shake 'em up and make 'em believe in ideals—yes, in themselves. But I get into a rut of teaching. I need young critical things like you to punch me up. Tell me, what are you reading?"

"I've been re-reading 'The Damnation of Theron Ware.' Do you know it?"

"Yes. It was clever. But hard. Man wanted to tear down, not build up. Cynical. Oh, I do hope I'm not a sentimentalist. But I can't see any use in this high-art stuff that doesn't encourage us day-laborers to plod on."

> *"I have only one good quality—overwhelming belief in the brains and hearts of our nation, our state, our town."*

Main streets

Street Scene, Stillwater, Minn.

Central Ave., Faribault, Minn.

Ensued a fifteen-minute argument about the oldest topic in the world: It's art but is it pretty? Carol tried to be eloquent regarding honesty of observation. Miss Sherwin stood out for sweetness and a cautious use of the uncomfortable properties of light. At the end Carol cried:

"I don't care how much we disagree. It's a relief to have somebody talk something besides crops. Let's make Gopher Prairie rock to its foundations: let's have afternoon tea instead of afternoon coffee."

Mrs. Bogart lived across the alley from the rear of Carol's house. She was a widow, and a Prominent Baptist, and a Good Influence. She had so painfully reared three sons to be Christian gentlemen that one of them had become an Omaha bartender, one a professor of Greek, and one, Cyrus N. Bogart, a boy of fourteen who was still at home, the most brazen member of the toughest gang in Boytown.

Mrs. Bogart was not the acid type of Good Influence. She was the soft, damp, fat, sighing, indigestive, clinging, melancholy, depressingly hopeful kind. There are in every large chicken-yard a number of old and indignant hens who resemble Mrs. Bogart, and when they are served at Sunday noon dinner, as fricasseed chicken with thick dumplings, they keep up the resemblance.

Carol had noted that Mrs. Bogart from her side window kept an eye upon the house. The Kennicotts and Mrs. Bogart did not move in the same sets—which meant precisely the same in Gopher Prairie as it did on Fifth Avenue or in Mayfair. But the good widow came calling.

She wheezed in, sighed, gave Carol a pulpy hand, sighed, glanced sharply at the revelation of ankles as Carol crossed her legs, sighed, inspected the new blue chairs, smiled with a coy sighing sound, and gave voice:

"I've wanted to call on you so long, dearie, you know we're neighbors, but I thought I'd wait till you got settled, you must run in and see me, how much did that big chair cost?"

"Seventy-seven dollars!"

"Sev—— Sakes alive! Well, I suppose it's all right for them that can afford it, though I do sometimes think—— Of course as our pastor said once, at Baptist Church—— By the way, we haven't seen you there yet, and of course your husband was raised up a Baptist, and I do hope he won't drift away from the fold, of course we all know there isn't anything, not cleverness or gifts of gold or anything, that can make up for humility and the inward grace and they can say what they want to about the P. E. church, but of course there's no church that has more history or has stayed by the true principles of Christianity better than the Baptist Church and—— In what church were you raised, Mrs. Kennicott?"

"W-why, I went to Congregational, as a girl in Mankato, but my college was Universalist."

"Well—— But of course as the Bible says, is it the Bible, at least I know I have heard it in church and everybody admits it, it's proper for the little bride to take her husband's vessel of faith, so we all hope we shall see you at the Baptist Church and—— As I was saying, of course I agree with Reverend Zitterel in thinking that the great trouble with this nation today is lack of spiritual faith—so few going to church, and people automobiling on Sunday and heaven knows what all. But still I do think that one trouble is this terrible waste of money, people feeling that they've got to have bathtubs and telephones in their houses—— I heard you were selling the old furniture cheap."

"Yes!"

"Well—of course you know your own mind, but I can't help thinking, when Will's ma was down here keeping house for him—*she* used to run in to *see* me, real *often!*—it was good enough furniture for her. But there, there, I mustn't croak, I just wanted to let you know that when you find you can't depend on a lot of these gadding young folks like the Haydocks and the Dyers—and heaven only knows how much money Juanita Haydock blows in a year—why then you may be glad to know that slow old Aunty Bogart is always right there, and heaven knows——" A portentous sigh. "—I *hope* you and your husband won't have any of the troubles, with sickness and quarreling and wasting money and all that so many of these young couples do have and—— But I must be running along now, dearie. It's been such a pleasure and—— Just run in and see me any time. I hope Will is well? I thought he looked a wee mite peaked."

It was twenty minutes later when Mrs. Bogart finally oozed out of the front door. Carol ran back into the living-room and jerked open the windows. "That woman has left damp finger-prints in the air," she said.

Goths
and Visigoths

By Jon Hassler

Like Sinclair Lewis, Jon Hassler wrote volumes about small-town Minnesota and its denizens, but from that starting point the two authors' styles differed radically. Where Lewis lanced small towns, Hassler understood and loved them. He wrote warmly—as well as with gentle humor—about his characters' foibles and limitations, their humanity and dreams.

Although Hassler was born in Minneapolis in 1933, he grew up in the town of Plainview. He taught high school in several other Minnesota burgs before moving on to teach at Bemidji State University, followed by Brainerd Community College. He began writing at the age of thirty-seven.

Hassler's first novel was *Staggerford* (1977), followed by several young adult novels as well as *Simon's Night* (1979), *The Love Hunter* (1981), *The Green Journey* (1985), *Grand Opening* (1987), *North of Hope* (1990), and *Dear James* (1993).

This excerpt from *Staggerford* presents one of Hassler's most memorable characters, the small-town schoolmarm Miss Agatha McGee, in all of her raging glory.

"ELEVATORS"
Minnesota artist Mac LeSueur's 1934 cubist oil painting of grain elevators evokes an iconic image of the small-town skyscrapers. (Minnesota Historical Society)

FEW COULD REMEMBER a time when Miss McGee—slight and splay-footed and quick as a bird—was not teaching at St. Isidore's. This was her forty-first year in the same classroom, her forty-first year of flitting and hovering up and down the aisles in the morning when she felt fresh, and perching behind her walnut desk in the afternoon when fatigue set in. In the minds of her former students, many of whom were now grandparents, she occupied a place somewhere between Moses and Emily Post, and when they met her on the street they guarded not only their speech but also their thoughts.

They knew of course—for she had been telling the story for over half a century—that when she was a girl she had met Joyce Kilmer, but who would have guessed the connection between that meeting many years ago and the fire alarm this afternoon? Standing in the garden among her cabbages, she decided that she would never tell a soul—not even Miles—about the cause of the fire alarm. She could not lie, but she could keep a secret.

She could not lie, but she could keep a secret.

Agatha McGee met Joyce Kilmer when she was six. She was a first grader at St. Isidore's. The year was 1916 and her teacher, Sister Rose of Lima, primed the first grade for months, leading them in a recitation of "Trees" every morning between the Apostles' Creed and the Pledge of Allegiance; and then on the last day of school before Christmas break, Joyce Kilmer stepped through the classroom door at the appointed hour, casting Sister Rose of Lima into a state of stuttering foolishness and her students into ecstasy. Miss McGee remembered it like yesterday. Mr. Kilmer was handsome, cheery, and a bit plump. He wore a black suit and a red tie. With a playful sparkle in his eye he bowed to Sister Rose of Lima, saying he was delighted to meet her, and then he walked among her students, asking their names. The children's voices were suddenly undependable, and they told their names in tense whispers and unexpected shouts. Jesse Farnham momentarily forgot who he was, and the silence was thick while he thought. When he finally said, "Jesse," Mr. Kilmer told him that he had known a girl by that name, and the first grade exploded with more laughter than Sister Rose of Lima permitted on ordinary days. (Priests and poets melted her severity.) The laughter, ending as suddenly as it began, was followed by a comfortable chat, the poet telling stories, some without lessons. Before Mr. Kilmer left, his admirers recited "Trees" for him. For Agatha McGee his visit was, like Christmas in those years, a joy undiminished by anticipation.

But that was long ago. Nowadays poetry, among other things, wasn't what it used to be. Yesterday at St. Isidore's as Miss McGee sat at the faculty lunch table she overheard Sister Rosie tell Sister Judy in an excited whisper that Herschel Mancrief was coming to town. He was touring the Midwest on a federal grant, and would arrive at St. Isidore's at ten the next morning. The two sisters were huddled low over the Spanish rice, trying to keep the news from Miss McGee. She wasn't surprised. She was well aware that the new nuns, although pranked out in permanents and skirts up to their knees, were still a clandestine sorority. How like them to plan an interruption in the schoolday and not let her know.

"About whom are you speaking?" she asked.

"Oh, Miss McGee," said Sister Rosie, the lighthearted (and in McGee's opinion, light-headed) principal of St. Isidore's. "We were discussing Herschel Mancrief, and we were not at all sure you would be interested." Sister Rosie was twenty-six and she had pierced earlobes.

"I will be the judge of my interests, if you please. Who is Herschel Mancrief?"

"He's a poet the younger generation is reading," said Sister Judy, blushing behind her acne. "We studied him in the novitiate."

"His credentials are super," said Sister Rosie.

"And he's coming to St. Isidore's? I might have been told. Will he visit classes or speak to an assembly?"

"He will visit classes. But of course no one is obliged to have him in. I know what a nuisance interruptions can be."

"Poets are important to children. I was visited by Mr. Joyce Kilmer when I was a girl, and I treasure the memory. Please show Mr. What's-his-name to my classroom when the time comes. What's his name?"

"Herschel Mancrief. He can give you twenty minutes at quarter to twelve."

So this morning Miss McGee announced to her sixth graders that they were about to meet Herschel Mancrief. They looked up from their reading assignment, a page headed "Goths and Visigoths," and as a sign of their undivided attention they closed their books. Divided attention was among the things Miss McGee did not permit. Slang and eye shadow were others.

"Meeting a poet is a memorable experience," she said. "When I was a girl, my class was visited by Mr. Joyce Kilmer, who wrote 'Trees,' the poem every child carries in his heart from the primary grades, and to this day I can recall what Mr. Kilmer said to us. He came to Staggerford a mere two years before giving his life for his country in World War One."

"COUNTY BAND CONCERT"
A summertime concert at the park band shell is captured in Minnesota artist Miriam Ibling's 1938 gouache-and-pencil illustration. (Minnesota Historical Society)

She tilted her head back, in order to read her twenty-four sixth graders through her bifocals—difficult reading these days, for they lurked, boys and girls alike, behind veils of hair.

"The poet, you understand, is a man with a message. His mission is to remind us of the beauty God has made. He writes of the good and lasting things of life. His business is beauty. Are there any questions?"

There was one, and several students raised their hands to ask it: "How does 'Trees' go?"

"Heavens, surely you remember."

But it was discovered that no one in the class had heard it. As Miss McGee began reciting, "'I think that I shall never see,'" a frightening sensation crept up her spine and gripped her heart—an invisible tremor like the one she had felt in 1918 when her third-grade teacher said that Joyce Kilmer was dead in France. An imperceptible shudder that moved out along her nervous system and left her nauseous. Her name for it was the Dark Age dyspepsia, because it struck whenever she came upon a new piece of alarming evidence that pointed to the return of the Dark Ages.

Dark Age evidence had been accumulating. Last month at Parents' Night, Barbara Betka's father and mother told Miss McGee they would see her fired if she did not lift her prohibition against the wearing of nylons by sixth-grade girls. They were standing in the assembly room where coffee was to be served. Mr. Betka, fidgeting and averting his eyes, did most of the talking while Mrs. Betka, having called the tune, stood at his side and fingered his arm like a musical instrument. "Fired indeed!" said Miss McGee, turning on her heel and snatching up her purse in a single motion of amazing agility, like a move in hopscotch, and she flew from the assembly room before coffee was served. She was followed home by the Dark Age dyspepsia and scarcely slept that night, haunted by the specter of a man in his fifties sent out by his wife to do battle for nylons. "The craven ninny," she said to herself at dawn, rising to prepare the day's lessons.

And that was the day Dr. Murphy from the State Department of Education came to town to address a joint meeting of public and parochial school faculties. Both Miles and Miss McGee attended his lecture. "Never," Dr. Murphy said at the end of a tedious address on language arts, "never burden a child with a book written earlier than the child's date of birth. That way you can be confident that you and your students are in tune with each other, that you are moving with them

MORNING SUN
Lanesboro basks in the first sunshine of the day. (Photograph © Layne Kennedy)

"First State Prison"
Josephine Lutz Rollins was a prolific Minnesota painter who had a long career teaching art at the University of Minnesota. She established the Stillwater Art Colony summer art school in the 1930s, founded the cooperative West Lake Gallery with a group of women artists in Minneapolis in 1965, and remained active as a painter and role model for younger women in the arts. This undated oil painting shows Minnesota's premier state prison at Stillwater. (Minnesota Historical Society)

on a contemporary plane." This harebrained proposal proved to Miss McGee that not even the State Department of Education was immune from the spreading plague of dark and crippling ignorance.

Nor were the sisters immune. More than once, for their spring picnic, Sister Judy had taken her fourth graders to a hippie farm. When Miss McGee first heard about that, she went to the pastor, Father Finn, and warned him about the return of the Dark Ages. Father Finn, ordinarily a man of understanding, did not understand Miss McGee's anxiety. If the Dark Ages were coming back, he had not yet caught sight of them. He told Miss McGee that she was an alarmist.

This morning as she concluded with the line, "But only God can make a tree," the door opened and Herschel Mancrief appeared. He was led into the classroom by Sister Rosie. He was untidy. That was Miss McGee's first impression of him. Under his wrinkled suitcoat he wore a T-shirt and under his nose a thicket of hair that curled around the corners of his mouth and ended in a stringy gray beard.

Miss McGee said, "I am pleased to meet you," and she gracefully offered her hand.

"Groovy," said the poet, tapping her palm with the tip of one finger. Up close she saw that his neck and his T-shirt were unmistakably unwashed. His asymmetrical sideburns held lint. She hopped silently backward and slipped into an empty desk halfway down an aisle, and Sister Rosie introduced the visitor, training a spit curl as she spoke.

"Mr. Mancrief has already been to three rooms and he has another one to visit after yours, class, and he has to leave by twelve thirty, so when his time is up please don't bug him to stay." On her way out the door, Sister Rosie added, "Room 102 is next, Herschel. It's just across the hall."

The sixth grade regarded the poet.

"I am here to make you childlike," he began, blinking as he spoke, as though his words gave off too much light. "I am here to save you from growing up." His voice was deep and wheezy, and his frown was fixed. "You see, grownups aren't sensitive. They get covered over with a kind of crust. They don't feel. It is only through constant effort that I am able to maintain the wonder, the joy, the capacity for feeling that I had as a child." He quit blinking and inserted a hand under his suitcoat to give his ribs a general and thoughtful scratching. "Do you understand what I am saying?"

The class looked at Miss McGee. She nodded and so did they.

"But poetry takes all of life for her domain. The beautiful and the unbeautiful. Roses and toilets. Today's poet seeks to represent the proportions of life. You don't very often pick a rose, but you go to the bathroom several times a day."

"Good. Now here's a poem of mine called 'What I Envied.' It's an example of what I'm saying." He closed his eyes and spoke in an altered voice, a chant:

"I envied as a child
the clean manikins in store windows
because their underwear fit
their toes were buried in thick carpet
their happy smiles immutable,
until my father driving us home
past midnight after a day in the country
passed a window full of manikins
and then I knew
the trouble it must be
to smile all night!"

After a silent moment the poet opened his eyes signaling the end of the poem.

Miss McGee had heard worse. Except for the reference to underwear, it came as close to poetry as most of the verse she had read lately, and she set the class to nodding its approval.

Herschel Mancrief shed his suitcoat and revealed that his pants were held up by a knotted rope. It was not the white, carefully braided rope of the Franciscans, who were Miss McGee's teachers in college, but a dirty length of frazzled twine.

"Good," said the poet, laying his suitcoat across Miss McGee's walnut desk. "You remember how heroic those manikins used to seem when you were small and they were larger than life. You would see one in a store window and it was enough to make you salute. The pity is that you gradually lose your sense of wonder for things like that. Take toilets, for example. My poem 'So Tall' is about a toilet."

He recited with his eyes shut. Miss McGee shut hers as well.

"How tall I seem to be these days
and how much I am missing,
things at ground level escape my notice
wall plugs wastebaskets heat registers,
what do I care for them now I am so tall?
I was once acquainted with a toilet
when it and I were eye to eye,
it would roar and swallow and scare me half to death.
What do I care for that toilet now,

now I am so tall?"

There was the sound of a giggle, stifled.

"You are surprised I got a toilet into a poem?" He was asking Miss McGee, who had not giggled. "But poetry takes all of life for her domain. The beautiful and the unbeautiful. Roses and toilets. Today's poet seeks to represent the proportions of life. You don't very often pick a rose, but you go to the bathroom several times a day."

Certain now that he had taken the measure of Miss McGee's tolerance for the unbeautiful (color was rising in her face) the poet announced his third selection, "In My End of Town."

"In my end of town
like a cathedral against the sky
stands the city sewage plant,
the direction of the wind
is important to us,
in my end of town
man disposes."

He opened his eyes to study Miss McGee's reaction, but the desk she had been sitting in was empty. She was at his side, facing the class.

"Students, you will thank Mr. Mancrief."

"Thank you, Mr. Mancrief." They spoke the way they prayed, in unison and without enthusiasm.

She handed the poet his coat and, not wishing to touch his hairy arms, she steered him to the door as if by remote control. "There"—she pointed—"is Room 102."

Nothing in his government-sponsored travels had prepared Herschel Mancrief for the brush-off. "Actually," he said, blinking as he backed into the corridor, "I hadn't finished."

"I regret we can spare you no more time. We recite the Angelus at twelve."

Looking more surprised than offended, he raised a hand as though to speak, but then thought better of it and stepped across the corridor and knocked on the door of 102. It opened instantly and Sister Judy put her head out.

Miss McGee, afraid now that her treatment of the man had been too delicate, said, "Another thing, Mr. Mancrief. Your poetry is . . ." She searched for the word. The poet and Sister Judy listened for it.

"Your poetry is undistinguished."

Sister Judy rolled her eyes and the poet chuckled into his hand. Miss McGee turned back to her class, pulling the door shut behind her. "Entirely undistinguished, class. You will rise now for the Angelus."

Later, entering the lunchroom, Miss McGee saw at the far end of the faculty table Herschel Mancrief and Sister Judy ignoring their beans and tuna and laughing like ninnies.

"I thought he was to have been on his way by this time."

"We asked him to stay for lunch," said Sister Rosie "He has agreed to stay a while longer. Isn't he super?"

"He's horribly dated. He said 'groovy.' I haven't heard anyone say 'groovy' for at least three years."

"Oh, Miss McGee, he's super. Admit it."

"Pass the relish, if you please."

Two hours later, after putting her class to work on equilateral triangles, Miss McGee opened her door for a change of air. From behind the closed door of 102 she heard raucous laughter alternating with the excited voice of Herschel Mancrief. The man evidently could not bring himself to leave St. Isidore's. She stepped closer and listened through the door.

"Acquainted with a toilet," said the poet.

The fourth grade laughed.

"It would roar and swallow and scare me half to death."

More laughter.

"There, now you've caught the spirit of the poem. Now repeat it after me."

They did so, briskly, line by line.

"Now let's try another one—a poem I wrote just the other day called 'Be Careful Where You Grab Me.'"

Fierce laughter.

Miss McGee hurried to the nearest fire alarm and with a trembling hand she broke the seal and set off an ear-splitting jangle of horns and bells that emptied the building in forty-five seconds. Two ladder trucks pulled up to the front door and while the fire chief, a former student of Miss McGee's, gave the building a thorough inspection, Herschel Mancrief drove off in his rented car, the fourth grade throwing him kisses from the curb.

"A false alarm," declared the fire chief, emerging from the front door of the school in his yellow rubber coat.

"Someone set off the alarm near your room," he said to Miss McGee as she led her sixth grade up the steps and back into the building. "Did you notice anything suspicious, Miss McGee?"

"Goths and Visigoths," she said.

GENERAL STORE
The Bay Store on Lake of the Woods has been serving its faithful customers for decades in the tried-and-true fashion of the old time general store. (Photograph © Layne Kennedy)

Life

Is Good

By Garrison Keillor

Garrison Keillor needs little introduction. He is the host and writer of the public radio show "A Prairie Home Companion," which is modeled on the "Grand Ole Opry" and other radio shows of yesteryear that kept farm families company after a day of hard work.

Born in Anoka in 1942, Keillor became fascinated by the *New Yorker* magazine during high school and strove to be published in its pages. While honing his craft as a writer, he also worked for Minnesota Public Radio, which would later become the home of "A Prairie Home Companion."

Keillor is the author of numerous books, some of which grew out of his radio show and its semi-fictional hometown, Lake Wobegon. Among his books are *Happy to Be Here* (1982), *Lake Wobegon Days* (1985), *Leaving Home* (1987), *We Are Still Married* (1989), *WLT: A Radio Romance* (1991), *The Book of Guys* (1993), and *Wobegon Boy* (1997).

Keillor originally presented this monologue on "A Prairie Home Companion"; it was collected in *Leaving Home.*

MINNESOTA HOT DISHES BY REGION

Minnesota's principal hot dishes are cataloged by region in this cuisine cartography created by Faye Passow.

IT HAS BEEN a quiet week in Lake Wobegon. Lightning struck the Tollerud farm Tuesday, about six o'clock in the evening. Daryl and his dad were walking the corn rows, talking, and the clouds were dark and strange but it wasn't storming yet, and Daryl said, "If I were you, I'd take Mother out to Seattle tomorrow and enjoy the trip and not worry about this." Right then it hit, up by the house: a burst of light and a slam and a sizzle like bacon. They ran for the house to find her in the kitchen, sitting on the floor. She was okay but it was close. It hit a crab apple tree thirty feet from the kitchen window.

Some people in town were reminded of Benny Barnes, who was hit by lightning six times. After three, he was nervous when a storm approached, and got in his car and drove fast, but it got him the fourth time, and the fifth time it was sunny with just one little cloud in the sky and, *bam*, lightning again. He had burn scars down his legs and his ears had been ringing for years. After the fifth, he quit running. The sixth one got him sitting in the yard on an aluminum lawn chair. After that he more or less gave up. When the next thunderstorm came through, he took a long steel pipe and stood out on the hill, holding it straight up. He had lost the will to live. But just the same it took him fifteen more years to die. It wasn't from lightning: he caught cold from the rain and died of pneumonia.

Daryl wished the bolt had come closer to his dad. His dad has a character flaw that drives Daryl crazy: he hates plans. The trip to Seattle was planned before Thanksgiving, letters were written to relatives, calls were made; June 30th was the date set to go, but the old man gets uneasy when plans are made and feels trapped and cornered, even if the plans are his own, so one night after chores he said, "Well, I don't know about that trip to Seattle, I might be too busy, we'll have to see about that," which made everybody else want to shoot him.

Daryl jumped up. "How can you say that? Are you crazy?" No, just nervous about plans. Always was. To agree to do something and have people expect you to do it: it bothers him. When his kids were little, he'd tell them, "Now, I'm not promising anything, but maybe next week sometime I could take you swimming, up to your uncle Carl's, but don't count on it, it all depends." As next week came around, he'd say, "I don't know about that swimming, we're going to have to see about that. Maybe Thursday." Thursday the kids would get their bathing suits out and he'd say, "We'll see how it goes this morning, if I get my work done we'll go." Right up to when they got in the car, he was saying, "I don't know. I really ought to get to work on that drain pipe," and even when he stuck the key in the ignition, he'd hesitate. "Gosh, I'm not sure, maybe it'd be better if we went tomorrow." He couldn't bring himself to say, "Thursday we swim," and stick to it. Daryl and his brothers and sisters learned not to look forward to things because Dad might change his mind.

The old man is the same with his grandkids. He says, "Well, we'll see. Maybe. If I can." But the Seattle trip beats all. Ruby got the train tickets and had the suitcase packed three weeks ago, then he said, "I don't know how I can leave with the corn like it is." Ruby put her head in her hands. He said, "You know, the Grand Canyon is a place I always wanted to see, maybe we should go there." She sighed, and he said, "You know, I never agreed to this Seattle trip, this was your idea from day one." And then Ruby went to Daryl's to talk to Daryl and Marilyn. They sat drinking coffee and getting madder and Ruby said, "Oh well, you have to understand Dad." Marilyn stood up and said, "I do not have to understand him. He's crazy. He doesn't just have a screw loose, the whole top has come off."

She is reading a book, *Get Down and Garden,* about getting tough with plants. She has yanked a bunch of slow movers out of her flower garden, the dullards and the dim bulbs, and it's improved her confidence. Now she often begins sentences with "Look," as in "Look. It's obvious." She used to begin with "Well," as in "Well, I don't know," but now she says, "Look. This is not that hard to understand,"

She said to Ruby, "Look. It's obvious what he's doing. He wants to be the Grand Exalted Ruler and come down in the morning and hear his subjects say, 'What is your pleasure, sire?' and he'll say, 'Seattle,' so they head for the luggage and then he says, 'No, we'll stay home,' so they sit down, and then 'Grand Canyon' and they all jump up. As long as you keep jumping, he'll keep holding the hoop up there."

Not only does Old Man Tollerud hate to commit himself to trips, he also likes to stay loose in regard to drawing up a will or some other legal paper that gives Daryl and Marilyn some right to the farm that they've worked on for fifteen years. When Daryl mentions it, his dad says, "Well, we'll have to see. We'll talk about it in a few months." Daryl is forty-two years old and he's got no more ownership of this farm than if he'd gone off and been a drunk like his brother Gunnar. Sometimes he gets so mad at the old man, he screams at him. But always when he's on the tractor in the middle of

MINNESOTA FISHERMEN
Armed with their handy travel-sized fishing rods and reels, two Minnesota anglers prepare for a day chasing the big catch. Moorhead photographer Wayne Gudmundson has chronicled life in Minnesota with a wry eye in his numerous books of images, including Minnesota Gothic, Common Water, *and* Crossings: A Photographic Document of Fargo, North Dakota. *(Photograph © Wayne Gudmundson)*

ABOVE: **A MAN AND HIS COW**
A farmer's best friend. (Minnesota State Fair collection)

OPPOSITE PAGE: **HOT DATE**
A young couple tries out the ergonomics of the latest in John Deere tractor offerings at the Minnesota State Fair's machinery hill in the 1930s. (Minnesota State Fair collection)

the field with the motor running. Once he left a rake in the yard with the tines up, hoping his dad would step on it and brain himself.

Last April he saw a skunk waddling toward the barn and got a can of catfood and lured the skunk into the tractor shed, hoping his dad would start up the John Deere the next morning and get a snootful. He fed the skunk day after day, waiting for it to do the job for him. Sweet justice. Blast the old bastard with skunk sauce at close range so nobody would care to see him for about a year. Then the skunk started following Daryl, who fed him such rich food, so Daryl quit and the skunk disappeared.

Daryl got some satisfaction at the Syttende Mai dinner at the Lutheran church in May, Norwegian Independence Day, where his dad went through the buffet and loaded up and was heading for a table when his paper plate started to collapse on him. He balanced his coffee cup on his wrist to get his other hand under the plate, and it was *hot*—the meatballs had sat in a chafing dish over a candle. The old man winced and looked for a place to dump the load; then the hot gravy burned right through the paper plate and he did a little tango and everything sloshed down the front of his pants. Daryl watched this with warm satisfaction.

But that was months ago, the satisfaction has worn off. The day after the lightning strike, Daryl drove up to the house to have it out once and for all. He practiced his speech in the pickup. "You don't treat me like I'm your son at all, you've never treated me like a son." He got to the house and found a note on the door: "Gone to Saint Cloud for windowshades. Back soon. Clean the haybarn."

Clean the haybarn! He ripped the note off and wadded it up and drop-kicked it into the peonies. He stalked to the end of the porch and back and stood and yelled at the door: "You don't treat me like I was your son, you bastard, you treat me like I was a—" And then the terrible truth dawned on him. His mother had said, "If anything happens to us in Seattle, I left you a letter in my dresser drawer. I've been meaning to give it to you for years." So he wasn't their son. He was adopted. That's why his dad wouldn't make out the will.

Daryl had wondered about this before, if he was his father's son. He thought, "I'm forty-two, it's time to

find out." He walked in and climbed the stairs, step by deep purple step, and turned and entered his parents' bedroom, the forbidden chamber, and walked to the dresser and heard something move on the bed. He turned—it was their old tabby cat, Lulu, on the bed—his hand hit a bottle and it crashed on the floor. She didn't jump at the crash, she sat up and gave him a long look that said: "You're not supposed to be in here and you know it. You ought to be ashamed of yourself. You're no good, and you know it. Shame on you." He clapped his hands—*Ha! Git!*—and she climbed down and walked away, stopped, looked over her shoulder, and said: You'll suffer for this, you just wait.

He picked up the shards of perfume bottle and opened both dormer windows to air out the room. Unbelievable that his mother would ever smell like this, it smelled like old fruit salads. He dug down into the dresser drawer where he'd seen her stick old pictures, under her stockings and underwear. There was a book, *Sexual Aspects of Christian Marriage: A Meditation* by Reverend E. M. Mintner, that he'd read when he was twelve, and he dug beneath it to a packet of envelopes tied with a thick rubber binder, *tight*. He slipped it off: they were his dad's pay slips from the Co-op; each envelope held a year's worth; there were more than thirty envelopes.

He sat on the bed, feeling weak. Of all his parents' secrets, this was the darkest: how much money did they make? They would no more talk about that than discuss sexual aspects of marriage. One Sunday little Daryl piped up at dinner and

asked, "Dad, how much money do you make?"

His dad has several different voices, a regular one ("So how come you went down there then when I told you I needed you? I don't get it") and a prayer voice ("Our Father, we do come before Thee with hearts filled with thanksgiving, remembering Thy many blessings to us, and we do ask Thee now . . ."). When he discussed money he used the second voice and he said, "I don't care to discuss that and I don't want you to discuss it with anyone else. Is that clear?"

Oh yes. We don't talk about money, that is very clear. Except to say, "I got this window fan for four dollars; it's brand-new except for this scratch, and you know those things run ten, twelve dollars." Bargains yes, but salaries no.

So here was the secret. He opened the first envelope, 1956. Forty-five dollars. That was for a whole week. Not much for a good mechanic. Forty-five dollars and five kids: it explained all that scrimping, his mother darning socks and canning tomatoes. When the old man forked over their allowance, he counted the two quarters twice to make sure he wasn't overpaying. It explained why he was such a pack rat, saving tinfoil, string, paper, rags—once Daryl looked around for string and found a box full of corks, another of bits of wire, and one box with hundreds of odd jigsawpuzzle pieces, labeled "Puzzle: Misc."

It dawned on him that he wasn't adopted, he was their boy all right. He'd inherited their frugality and stoicism. If his paper plate fell apart, he'd try to save it, even if his hand was burning. Same as his dad. They raised him to bear up under hardship and sadness and disappointment and disaster, but what if you're brought up to be stoic and your life turns out lucky—you're in love with your wife, you're lucky in your children, and life is lovely to you— what then? You're ready to endure trouble and pain, and instead God sends you love—what do you do? He'd been worried about inheriting the farm, meanwhile God had given him six beautiful children. What happens if you expect the worst and you get the best? *Thank you, Lord,* he thought. Thank you for sending me up here to the bedroom. It was wrong to come, but thank you for sending me.

He heard Lulu tiptoe in, and when she brushed against his leg he was sorry for chasing her out. He scratched her head. It didn't feel catlike. He looked down and saw the white stripes down its back.

The skunk sniffed his hand, wondering where the catfood was. Then it raised its head and sniffed the spilled perfume. It raised its tail, sensing an adversary. It walked toward the window. It seemed edgy.

"Easy, easy," he said. If he opened the window wider, it might go out on the roof and find a route down the oak tree to the ground. He was opening the window wider when he heard the feet padding up the stairs. He hollered, "No, Shep, no!" and raised his leg to climb out the window as the dog burst into the room, barking. The skunk turned and attacked. Daryl went out the window, but not quite fast enough. He tore off all his clothes and threw them down to the ground, and climbed back in. The bedroom smelled so strong he couldn't bear it. The skunk was under the bed. He ran down and got the shotgun and loaded it. Daryl was almost dying of the smell, but he crept into the bedroom. He heard the skunk grunt, trying to squeeze out more juice. Daryl aimed and fired. Feathers exploded and the skunk dropped down dead.

He carried it out on a shovel and buried it, but that didn't help very much: the deceased was still very much a part of the Tollerud house when his parents arrived home a little while later. Daryl sat on the porch steps, bare naked except for a newspaper. He smelled so bad, he didn't care about modesty. Ruby said, "Oh dear. Are you all right?" She stopped, twenty feet away. She thought he looked naked, but he smelled so bad she didn't care to come closer.

His dad said, "You know, Daryl, I think you were right about Seattle."

And they left. They didn't take clothes with them. They went straight out the driveway.

That was Tuesday. Daryl has been living at his parents' house all week. But life is good. I'm sure he still believes this. Life is good, friends. It's even better if you stay away from Daryl, but basically life is good.

PAUL BUNYAN AND FRIEND
The legend of the gigantic lumberjack Paul Bunyan has inspired many a tall tale—as well as countless roadside attractions. This 1940s postcard shows a statue of Paul Bunyan (left) in Bemidji, one of approximately ten Bunyan statues in Minnesota, including six in Brainerd alone. In addition, Minnesota proudly boasts three statues of Babe the Blue Ox and twelve of Paul's personal effects, from his axe in Brainerd (naturally) to his CB radio in Bemidji. Other statues display his moccasins, razor, phone, footprint, mouth organ, shovel, and mailbox. His cradle can be found in Akeley and his grave in Kelliher.

The Romantic Egotist

By F. Scott Fitzgerald

Of all writers, Minnesotans often boast the most pride in Francis Scott Fitzgerald. The fact is, however, that while Fitzgerald was born and raised in Minnesota, few of his novels or short stories were based in the state. Still, throughout his roller coaster career and troubled life, he often returned to his home city of St. Paul as a refuge.

Fitzgerald's first novel, *This Side of Paradise* (1920), is a fascinating blend of humorous satire and autobiography that stunned readers of its day with its freshness, heralding a new era in American fiction. While this first book was a resounding success, Fitzgerald's following novels were initially commercial failures, including his masterpiece, *The Great Gatsby* (1925), a book so stunning that even Fitzgerald's best friend and chief rival, Ernest Hemingway, spoke kindly of it.

It was as a short story writer that Fitzgerald earned his keep, and his prolific outpouring of short fiction allowed him and his wife Zelda to live the fast life they desired. In his numerous books, Fitzgerald became the voice of the Jazz Age of the 1920s and the Lost Generation of expatriates based largely in Paris.

The following excerpt signalled the debut of Fitzgerald as a writer, coming from the opening pages of *This Side of Paradise.* It also presented a thinly veiled portrait of the artist as a young man—or at least of his vision of the young man he may have wished to be.

ICE CASTLE

The St. Paul Winter Carnival's ice castle shimmers before the city skyline. (Photograph © Bob Firth)

Amory Blaine inherited from his mother every trait, except the stray inexpressible few, that made him worth while. His father, an ineffectual, inarticulate man with a taste for Byron and a habit of drowsing over the Encyclopedia Britannica, grew wealthy at thirty through the death of two elder brothers, successful Chicago brokers, and in the first flush of feeling that the world was his, went to Bar Harbor and met Beatrice O'Hara. In consequence, Stephen Blaine handed down to posterity his height of just under six feet and his tendency to waver at crucial moments, these two abstractions appearing in his son Amory. For many years he hovered in the background of his family's life, an unassertive figure with a face half-obliterated by lifeless, silky hair, continually occupied in "taking care" of his wife, continually harassed by the idea that he didn't and couldn't understand her.

But Beatrice Blaine! There was a woman! Early pictures taken on her father's estate at Lake Geneva, Wisconsin, or in Rome at the Sacred Heart Convent—an educational extravagance that in her youth was only for the daughters of the exceptionally wealthy—showed the exquisite delicacy of her features, the consummate art and simplicity of her clothes. A brilliant education she had— her youth passed in renaissance glory, she was versed in the latest gossip of the Older Roman Families; known by name as a fabulously wealthy American girl to Cardinal Vitori and Queen Margherita and more subtle celebrities that one must have had some culture even to have heard of. She learned in England to prefer whiskey and soda to wine, and her small talk was broadened in two senses during a winter in Vienna. All in all Beatrice O'Hara absorbed the sort of education that will be quite impossible ever again; a tutelage measured by the number of things and people one could be contemptuous of and charming about; a culture rich in all arts and traditions, barren of all ideas, in the last of those days when the great gardener clipped the inferior roses to produce one perfect bud.

In her less important moments she returned to America, met Stephen Blaine and married him—this almost entirely because she was a little bit weary, a little bit sad. Her only child was carried through a tiresome season and brought into the world on a spring day in ninety-six.

When Amory was five he was already a delightful companion for her. He was an auburn-haired boy, with great, handsome eyes which he would grow up to in time, a facile imaginative mind and a taste for fancy dress. From his fourth to his tenth year he did the country with his mother in her father's private car, from Coronado, where his mother became so bored that she had a nervous breakdown in a fashionable hotel, down to Mexico City, where she took a mild, almost epidemic consumption. This trouble pleased her, and later she made use of it as an intrinsic part of her atmosphere—especially after several astounding bracers.

So, while more or less fortunate little rich boys were defying governesses on the beach at Newport, or being spanked or tutored or read to from "Do and Dare," or "Frank on the Mississippi," Amory was biting acquiescent bell-boys in the Waldorf, outgrowing a natural repugnance to chamber music and symphonies, and deriving a highly specialized education from his mother.

"Amory."

"Yes, Beatrice." (Such a quaint name for his mother; she encouraged it.)

"Dear, don't *think* of getting out of bed yet. I've always suspected that early rising in early life makes one nervous. Clothilde is having your breakfast brought up."

"All right."

"I am feeling very old to-day, Amory," she would sigh, her face a rare cameo of pathos, her voice exquisitely modulated, her hands as facile as Bernhardt's. "My nerves are on edge—on edge. We must leave this terrifying place to-morrow and go searching for sunshine."

Amory's penetrating green eyes would look out through tangled hair at his mother. Even at this age he had no illusions about her.

"Amory."

"Oh, *yes.*"

"I want you to take a red-hot bath—as hot as you can bear it, and just relax your nerves. You can read in the tub if you wish."

She fed him sections of the "Fêtes Galantes" before he was ten; at eleven he could talk glibly, if rather reminiscently, of Brahms and Mozart and Beethoven. One afternoon, when left alone in the hotel at Hot Springs, he sampled his mother's apricot cordial, and as the taste pleased him, he became quite tipsy. This was fun for a while, but he essayed a cigarette in his exaltation, and succumbed to a vulgar, plebeian reaction. Though this incident horrified Beatrice, it also secretly amused her and became part of what in a later generation would have been termed her "line."

"This son of mine," he heard her tell a room full of awe-struck, admiring women one day, "is entirely sophisticated and quite charming—but delicate—we're all delicate; *here,* you know." Her hand was radiantly outlined against her

> Amory Blaine inherited from his mother every trait, except the stray inexpressible few, that made him worth while.

"Winter Twilight"
Wanda Gág's undated lithograph captures the mood of a winter evening on a street in almost any Minnesota town or city. (Minnesota Historical Society)

beautiful bosom; then sinking her voice to a whisper, she told them of the apricot cordial. They rejoiced, for she was a brave raconteuse, but many were the keys turned in sideboard locks that night against the possible defection of little Bobby or Barbara. . . .

These domestic pilgrimages were invariably in state; two maids, the private car, or Mr. Blaine when available, and very often a physician. When Amory had the whooping-cough four disgusted specialists glared at each other hunched around his bed; when he took scarlet fever the number of attendants, including physicians and nurses, totalled fourteen. However, blood being thicker than broth, he was pulled through.

The Blaines were attached to no city. They were the Blaines of Lake Geneva; they had quite enough relatives to serve in place of friends, and an enviable standing from Pasadena to Cape Cod. But Beatrice grew more and more prone to like only new acquaintances, as there were certain stories, such as the history of her constitution and its many amendments, memories of her years abroad, that it was necessary for her to repeat at regular intervals. Like Freudian dreams, they must be thrown off, else they would sweep in and lay siege to her nerves. But Beatrice was critical about American women, especially the floating population of ex-Westerners

"They have accents, my dear," she told Amory, "not Southern accents or Boston accents, not an accent attached to any locality, just an accent"—she became dreamy. "They pick up old, moth-eaten London accents that are down on their luck and have to be used by some one. They talk as an English butler might after several years in a Chicago grand-opera company." She became almost incoherent—"Suppose—time in every Western woman's life—she feels her husband is prosperous enough for her to have—accent—they try to impress *me*, my dear—"

Though she thought of her body as a mass of frailties, she considered her soul quite as ill, and therefore important in her life. She had once been a Catholic, but discovering that priests were infinitely more attentive when she was in process of losing or regaining faith in Mother Church, she maintained an enchantingly wavering attitude. Often she deplored the bourgeois quality of the American Catholic clergy, and was quite sure that had she lived in the shadow of the great

Continental cathedrals her soul would still be a thin flame on the mighty altar of Rome. Still, next to doctors, priests were her favorite sport.

"Ah, Bishop Wiston," she would declare, "I do not *want* to talk of myself. I can imagine the stream of hysterical women fluttering at your doors, beseeching you to be sim*patico*"— then after an interlude filled by the clergyman—"but my mood—is—oddly dissimilar."

Only to bishops and above did she divulge her clerical romance. When she had first returned to her country there had been a pagan, Swinburnian young man in Asheville, for whose passionate kisses and unsentimental conversations she had taken a decided penchant—they had discussed the matter pro and con with an intellectual romancing quite devoid of soppiness. Eventually she had decided to marry for background, and the young pagan from Asheville had gone through a spiritual crisis, joined the Catholic Church, and was now—Monsignor Darcy.

"Indeed, Mrs. Blaine, he is still delightful company—quite the cardinal's right-hand man."

"Amory will go to him one day, I know," breathed the beautiful lady, "and Monsignor Darcy will understand him as he understood me."

Amory became thirteen, rather tall and slender, and more than ever on to his Celtic mother. He had tutored occasionally—the idea being that he was to "keep up," at each place "taking up the work where he left off," yet as no tutor ever found the place he left off, his mind was still in very good shape. What a few more years of this life would have made of him is problematical. However, four hours out from land, Italy bound, with Beatrice, his appendix burst, probably from too many meals in bed, and after a series of frantic telegrams to Europe and America, to the amazement of the passengers the great ship slowly wheeled around and returned to New York to deposit Amory at the pier. You will admit that if it was not life it was magnificent.

After the operation Beatrice had a nervous breakdown that bore a suspicious resemblance to delirium tremens, and Amory was left in Minneapolis, destined to spend the ensuing two years with his aunt and uncle. There the crude, vulgar air of Western civilization first catches him—in his underwear, so to speak.

MICKEY'S DINER
Mickey's Diner is a twentieth-century landmark that has changed little since the day in 1939 that it was shipped east by rail from the famous Jerry O'Mahony, Inc., diner manufacturer of Elizabeth, New Jersey, and set up to do business in St. Paul. It has been open twenty-four hours a day, 365 days a year ever since. Diners were largely an East Coast phenomena, so Mickey's is a rare true prefabricated diner situated this far west of the Atlantic—and one of only a handful of diners anywhere on the National Register of Historic Places. (Photograph © Bob Firth/ Firth Photo Bank)

Being Respectable

By Grace H. Flandrau

In 1923, Grace Hodgson Flandrau published a novel entitled *Being Respectable* that painted a deliciously barbed portrait of the upper crust elite of St. Paul. The response was a mixture of shock and outrage—so much so, in fact, that the book became a bestseller of its day and was quickly made into a movie.

Grace Hodgson was born in St. Paul in 1889, schooled in Paris, and later married to Blair Flandrau. Her upbringing and her social circle provided the ideal background material to satirize in a fashion that would have made her contemporaries F. Scott Fitzgerald and Sinclair Lewis proud. Along with *Being Respectable*, Flandrau also published several other novels, short story collections, and travelogues, including *Entranced* (1924), *Then I Saw the Congo* (1929), *Indeed This Flesh* (1934), and *Under the Sun* (1936).

The bulk of Flandrau's literary legacy was ironically at odds with her satirical masterpiece, however. She researched and wrote numerous historical accounts of the accomplishments of that most elite of Minnesotans, James J. Hill, and his Great Northern Railway, most of them in fact published by the railroad.

This excerpt from the opening of *Being Respectable* is classic Grace Flandrau. Her city of Columbia is a thinly disguised St. Paul, and her portrayal of its citzenry drips with biting humor.

"PORTRAIT OF HAZEL THORSON STOICK STOECKELER"
Josephine Lutz Rollins's portrait in oils of a fellow painter was made as a wedding present for Stoeckeler circa 1945. (Minnesota Historical Society)

MR. DARIUS CARPENTER, standing on his front porch, with his neat broadcloth overcoat buttoned close against the spring wind, had an air of extreme solidity; an air of fitting admirably his surroundings; of being where he belonged; of prosperity unshakable and without ostentation.

When in a now remote infancy he had been baptized Darius and his brother Homer, it had been the impression in the small Ohio town where they were born, that Ellie Carpenter was going in for Roman emperors in naming her brood. The designation of the third son as Hector strengthened this belief. But after these flights Ellie's history or spirit of adventure failed her. A fourth, fifth and—after an interval of girls—sixth son were named plain Tom, John, and Jim.

All of them, with the exception of Jim and of course Darius, were now dead—four men, three women and one girl—the girl Lily who had died when she was thirteen. Eight graves nicely kept in respectable cemeteries in Ohio, New York state and Minnesota were all that was left to show for the greater part of Ellie's devoted efforts as wife, mother and pioneer helpmate. Sometimes Darius thought of the eight graves and, remembering his mother, they did not seem enough. If children had been made by these brothers and sisters it would be different. Children justified, explained many things otherwise inexplicable. Darius believed that way, in logical sequences. Causes and effects. Logical thinking. There was a simple negotiable reason for all things—cosmic laws dexterously leapt about proving human equations.

Children of course, did not always do their part toward establishing this justification. Then some other must be found. He himself, to be sure, had nothing to complain of. Deborah, perhaps, was a little difficult. She had ideas. But when she found a good husband she would get over them. People got over ideas. Louisa was satisfactory, carrying on those things Darius himself stood for—regularity, prominence in the community. And Charles's good news was profoundly gratifying. Darius thought of Charles with a deep and pious satisfaction.

He paused, before descending the steps, to take stock of the weather, having reached that time of life when weather inevitably becomes interesting. Moreover, in the northwest, weather is more than just weather. It is crops, mortgages, interest rates, prosperity, and panic—matters important to and deeply understood by Darius. But it was too early in the season for all that, and he observed with merely routine interest that the wind was from the east, that rain or possibly snow threatened, that spring would be later this year than usual.

Possessively, too, he observed these things. The state, its soil, history, flavor, and future seemed in some way specially his—loyalties which culminated in his feeling for the city. He knew all about the city—the things men do know about cities that grow up during their lifetime—cities they have, indeed, made. He was intimately a part of its financial and social institutions. In the early days he had held office. He had been mayor twice and postmaster. That was before Columbia was big enough to fall into the inevitable hands of political gangsters

He descended the steps, slowly examining, as his habit was, the well-manured grass beginning to turn green (it was the first grass on the avenue to turn green) and his budding trees. Darius was fond of trees. He knew every tree in the neighborhood individually as one knows persons or dogs, and interested himself in its condition and welfare. Only the night before he had called up Cy Pomfret to tell him his oaks needed attention.

He walked down the sidewalk with the upright, short-stepped walk of a prosperous, elderly man becoming stout. He proceeded deliberately, slapped the bole of a favorite elm with his cane, speared a stray piece of paper that was doing a tarantella across the lawn, poked at the straw over his tulip border.

A second flight of steps took him to the street where his shiny Cadillac sedan, a car redolent of common sense, waited for him. The driver wore the discreet semi-uniform favored in sensible Columbia. Like the car, Darius, and all the rest of it, he had a look of profound, unostentatious solvency. He greeted Darius with respectable affection, facetiously observing that they were having a pleasant winter that spring. Darius smiled, refusing to be helped to his seat. The man put a rug about his knees and slammed the door. The car slipped silently up the avenue. Darius sat with his hands folded over his cane, his eyes observant, through the shining panes, of the houses, trees, shrubbery they passed—so well known to him. Any alteration—a newly clipped hedge, a bit of building, interested him. The property of his friends was as vital to him as his own.

St. Andrew's stood on the corner of a quiet street—a respectable street—a street which in summer, when the oaks and elms were in full leaf, would even be beautiful. Now there was nothing to mitigate the varied ugliness of the houses—all of about the same and worst period; the period of frame

Darius believed that way, in logical sequences. Causes and effects. Logical thinking. There was a simple negotiable reason for all things—cosmic laws dexterously leapt about proving human equations.

"Frozen Mississippi"
Philip Little's 1909–1912 oil painting captures all of the chill of a frigid Minnesota winter day. (Minnesota Historical Society)

construction, cupolas, porticoes and fretwork. Some, indeed, shorn of their trimmings, had undergone a modernization in the form of a cement bath from which they emerged fantastic—the nightmare mud pie of a child who has eaten too many bananas.

The church rose chaste among them, secure in its Gothic lines. This Sunday morning it was the center of converging activity. Cars swept up to the curb. There was the snuffle of engines, the remote squealing of the organ, the tap of heels on cement walk, the subdued but festive sound of human voices in the open air.

Groups approached slowly. Husbands and wives, clean, dressed up, conscious of being clean and dressed up—of being on their way to church as is right and proper. An acuter

rectitude enveloping those who arrived on foot than those who arrived in motor cars—a satisfaction reminiscent perhaps of the time when it was not, in Columbia, considered delicate to go to church in an automobile. Women gloved and faintly rustling; men straight in morning coats, heads up, carrying polished canes—prominent citizens in every fiber—conscious perhaps, or subconscious, of their proper, pleasant backgrounds of piety, bank accounts, children, and positions in society. A flavor, it might be, of mild smugness inevitable, surely, to so happy an array of auspicious circumstance.

Louisa Denby, Darius's elder daughter, descending from her town car, was impressive. She was an ugly woman elaborately but fashionably dressed. She was accompanied by a

pretty little girl, a young-lady-like little girl, elaborately but fashionably dressed. They stood together on the grass near the curb stone, waiting for Darius.

Louisa suggested a tropical bird. Her hat was gay, her nose slightly beaked. It had received an ill-considered dose of powder before she left the car and loomed unnaturally white against the sallowness of her cheeks. They were guiltless of rouge, which Louisa considered immoral. This taboo, however, did not extend to lip-paint, and a streak of carmine outlined her thin lips. She was invested with a determined vivacity.

The droning squeal of the organ continued, and the subdued staccato of voices. Coming out, after "services," the congregation would talk louder. Louisa's rather wide mouth was stretched to a continual smile. The rich cherries and nameless vermilion-colored spikes on her hat bobbed incessantly in response to repeated congratulations. . . . "We think it's too splendid about Charles" . . . "perfectly lovely" . . . "too delightful," . . . and so on.

The little girl Millicent fixed inscrutable eyes on the faces passing above her, making no response to benevolent adult smiles. She managed to convey an awareness, by no means uncritically admiring, of each woman's costume and appearance.

The Cadillac, moving sedately up the avenue, dove suddenly sideways to the curb and ranged neatly alongside. The driver swung off the seat, and Louisa, too, proffered help to Darius which he did not want.

"Harry needn't come back, Papa. The Pierce is coming.'

Darius stood for a moment with his daughter. "Didn't they put it well in the paper?" she laughed. "I was really proud to come to church." Louisa was terribly vivacious when she talked, her mouth smiling widely. And she laughed a great deal, not humorously, but for something to do, as some people clear their throats.

Darius nodded. He had become silent of late years.

"Helen Davidson's cousin knows her and says she's perfectly *love*-ly." Louisa stressed adjectives and adverbs out of all reason—"She doesn't know Mrs. Schuyler Leyden or the Countess, but of course—" She suspended here on a sharp, vehement smile. All this was so exquisitely pleasant to Louisa that she forgot to laugh.

Millicent had been obliquely, as it were—attentive, looking slantwise away from them. When her contemporaries passed she greeted them with a certain remoteness. Although her conception of a countess must have been far from

definite, Millicent was aware of an asset not shared by the members of her world. But she was tired of hearing about it; she was tired of hearing her mother talk, she wished they would go in. Suddenly she exclaimed in a shrill, unexpected voice:

"Grampa, you've got long hairs on your hand. Oh! and there are brown spots, too."

"Millicent!" Her mother frowned lovingly. Darius hastily replaced the glove he had taken off. They move toward the church, mounted the steps, and pushed through the felt-covered swinging doors. A strong smell of varnish and plush, thinly sweetened with lilies, greeted them. The muffled squeal of the organ became loud and sonorous. Darius removed his hat.

An air of propriety enveloped his daughter Louisa. They walked up the aisle, waved forward by an elderly vestryman unspeakably correct in morning coat and striped breeches— eyeglasses, linen and bald spot all gleaming in the dim, painted light. No need, his gesture seemed to say, to show Mr. Carpenter or his daughter Mrs. Philip Denby to their seats; as well offer to guide St. Peter about Paradise. All three knelt a moment—Millicent, who enjoyed the pose, holding it till prodded by her mother.

"We have so much to be thankful for," Louisa whispered to her father, as they sat back. She smiled piously, thinking of Charles.

The smells, colors, sounds, the usual soothing atmosphere of church took Darius to its arms. Darius had nothing of the mystic. No nameless raptures were connected, for him, with the worship of Divinity. Worship, indeed, would by no means apply to what he experienced for a Being whom he respectfully alluded to as the Creator, nor to the emotions that brought him to his nicely cushioned pew each Sunday. He used the term, to be sure—but not as the lustrous word it is, thrown off white hot from some violence of human experience and hitched, since man became literate, democratic, and safe, to God knows what dreary soul squeezings.

He came to church because he found there, it seemed to him, the common sense so obviously wanting in the outside world—food for the logical mind—the obvious conception of right living. Do right and you will be rewarded: do wrong and sooner or later the thunderbolt will seek you out.

The curate was reading the commandments. . . . Thou shalt not steal, or lie. . . . Thou shalt not commit adultery. . . . It was all so simple, Darius thought, almost angrily. People only had to hear and obey.

MINNEHAHA FALLS
Framed by frost-coated trees, Minnehaha Falls glistens on a cold winter day. (Photograph © Richard Hamilton Smith)

God

By Evelyn Fairbanks

Evelyn Fairbanks was born in 1928 and raised in the famous black community of St. Paul's Rondo district. In the 1960s, the contentious construction of U.S. Interstate 94 destroyed the Rondo region, erasing a whole world in all but memory. Fairbanks's affectionate memoir, *The Days of Rondo* (1990), revived that time and place. Her firsthand account of life on Rondo created a living, breathing image of a vibrant community that was the heart of St. Paul's largest black neighborhood.

Fairbanks's reminiscences of days gone by range from memories of her family to school, summer camp to the war years. The stories tell of a community that was often independent of the white society around it.

In this chapter, Fairbanks writes about God, church, Sunday doings—and eating, one of the few good things in life that was not a sin and was thus given considerable attention.

CHURCH
The last light of the day shines on an empty church near Minneota. (Photograph © Bob Firth/Firth Photo Bank)

I'VE ALWAYS KNOWN about God. As far back as I can remember, God has been a part of my life, because God was the most important part of Mama's life. At first God was in Reverend Nelson's Sanctified church downtown, and then he moved to Reverend Callender's church on Central, and then he was at Reverend Lawrence's church on Chatsworth and Rondo, and that's where he remained until Mama died when I was eight.

Daddy didn't go to church, but Mama and I went all the time. On Wednesdays and Fridays there were prayer meetings and people gave testimony as to how God had uplifted them and changed their lives for the better. It was clear to me as a child that everyone in our church was happy, and even now as I look back (with what I assume is more sophistication) I don't remember anyone telling of hardships without adding, "But, thank God, I've still got my health and strength (or my job, or my family, or my right mind)." It seemed that whatever God took away, "in His goodness and mercy," He always left the most important thing behind.

We always had church all day on Sunday. First there was Sunday school, where we learned stories about people in the Bible, especially Jesus. We memorized verses in the Bible. That came in handy at the dinner table every evening, because everyone had to say a Bible verse by heart except Mama, who got to make up her own prayer. Even Daddy said a Bible verse. When we had company and the Bible verses, sometimes entire passages, got too long, Daddy would always say the shortest one in the Bible, "Jesus wept." I would snicker and Mama would give Daddy and me one of her warning glances. And in Sunday school we learned the songs that we sang sometimes for the grownups in church service. At least, the rest of the Sunday school got to sing sometimes. I got to sing almost every Sunday, because I was "Our Little Soloist" in Reverend Lawrence's church.

In the Sanctified church, the grooming of the church Soloist starts at a very early age. During my youth there were four active Soloists at one time. The Senior Soloist was a man or woman who grew up in the church (usually with a few years' absence to serve the Devil) and who, at one time, had a beautiful voice. But the Senior Soloist's voice could no longer reach the high, or the low, notes. Out of respect for advanced years and loyalty to the church, the Senior Soloist remained in that position until death.

It was extremely easy to get the back of your mother's hand across your face if you started to laugh at a missed note.

The Soloist was a person between thirty and forty years of age who usually read music, sometimes directed the choir, and remained in this position until she or he "graduated" to Senior Soloist. If the Soloist was a woman, she was also the person most likely to run off with the preacher.

The Junior Soloist category had the most turnover. These were young people in their late teens and early twenties who had been groomed, coached, and praised since they were the Little Soloist. Their voices and showmanship were nearly professional. Unfortunately, they were also in the prime years to serve the Devil.

Little Soloists were chosen for their big voices, willingness to perform, and encouraging parents (commonly known as stage mothers). I met all three requirements. In fact, I was so willing to perform that in the summer months I would stand on the top of the steps by the sidewalk and sing at the top of my voice, with a depth of feeling and freedom of spirit known only to children, loved children. So I was the Little Soloist.

My mind wandered while Reverend Lawrence was preaching, but he always got my attention when he interrupted his sermon to say, "I think I feel like hearing our Little Soloist sing a song."

When that happened, my mother got a very serious look on her face as she sat up even taller than usual and did something to my dress. She either straightened the ribbon in my hair, tied my belt again, or brushed my face with her hand to wipe something away. When she was through with me, I would squeeze past her lap (it felt so good to be close to my mother) and walk up the aisle while Reverend Lawrence quoted the verse about "Suffer little children to come unto me" or "Lest we become as children."

It seemed that I knew all of the words to all of the songs so anything that Sister Lawrence started to play, I would sing. My favorite was "In the Garden." I used to daydream about meeting God in the garden and we would have a lot of fun playing house together. I loved to play house, but seldom had anyone to play with. Mama didn't allow me to play with any of the children in the neighborhood because their parents were not Saved. I played only with other children at church or when the Sisters of the church were visiting us with their children.

Our activities were somewhat limited, because movies, dancing, and any game that required cards or dice were sinful and the punishment was immediate. But we were children like other children, with the same energies and curiosities. So we managed to have normal childhoods—although we learned to act like "little angels" in front of adults, as well as how to keep ourselves entertained during enforced solitude.

When I got through singing there were a lot of calls—"Amen," "Work through her, Jesus," and "Thank you, Jesus." Clapping, as a sign of appreciation, was considered worldly, but the calls gave the performer the same sense of satisfaction. I went back to my seat somehow closer to God and certainly closer to Mama.

As soon as church services were over, the mood began to shift from solemn joyousness to joyous activity. It was time for the Sunday dinner. Since eating was one of the few things in life that was not a sin according to our church laws, considerable attention was given to it.

The men took off their suit jackets and handed them to their wives to be folded neatly and placed on the back of the pews. We children giggled when we saw a young single man hand his jacket to one of the young ladies. That was our clue that they were "seeing" each other and therefore should be watched very closely, especially if they thought they were alone.

The men then started to set up the tables and folding chairs in the dining area, where we had Sunday school and Young People's Willing Workers (YPWW—like Sunday school for older children).

We children stood in front of our parents for instructions. The instructions were always the same, but we knew better than to leave without them. "Don't be running up and down the sidewalk. Don't get dirty. Stay where you can hear me. Stay out of people's way."

One time I did "run up and down the sidewalk" and I fell and broke my knee. All the other children stood around and looked at me, afraid to tell, because we had all been running up and down the sidewalk. Finally Mama came out 'cause she heard me hollering. She carried me into the church so that Reverend Callender could pray over the knee. He prayed over it for a week but it only got worse. Finally, Mama took me to the doctor and we found out that something was broken. I had plenty of time to stay in bed and think about what God did to children who didn't mind their parents.

Each Sunday after the children were out of the way, the women got their picnic baskets. On top were always their best bib aprons, freshly washed, starched, and ironed. (There was always a delay to admire a new apron, made since last Sunday.) Then came the freshly laundered tablecloths. These were the second-best tablecloths. The best were kept for when the preacher came to dinner. Some of these tablecloths had holes in them, but they were boiled, bleached, and rinsed in bluing. I never saw a spot on a tablecloth for Sunday dinner.

The food was brought out of the bottom of the basket with the seriousness of a sacrifice. And for good reason. It was almost always perfectly prepared. Spotless laundry and superb cooking were two skills expected among the church women. I remember how ruthlessly Florence Wilson was teased, for several Sundays, because her candied yams were too dry.

Besides candied yams there were greens, alone or mixed—collard, turnip, mustard, and dandelion—cooked with salt pork, bacon ends, or ham, which produced the pot likker that Daddy was so crazy about. There were navy, northern, or green beans, or black-eyed peas, also cooked with salt pork, bacon ends, or ham.

There was always chicken. It was fried or smothered in gravy or baked. If the chicken was baked, there was cornbread dressing. And there was ham and sometimes beef or pork roast. In season there was rabbit, squirrel, and fish. For dessert there were layered cakes with homemade jelly filling; fruit pies with crust that really did melt in your mouth; lemon meringue pies with peaks, valleys, and caves displaying a rainbow of browns; sweet potato pies, each made from a different recipe; and my favorite—peach cobbler. And there were jars and jars of homemade relishes made from cucumbers, tomatoes, onions, green and red peppers, beets, and watermelon rind.

The children sat at tables separate from the grown-ups. But there were at least two pairs of eyes on us at all times. None of us had to be told not to embarrass our parents. That was a mistake you made only once.

At the grown-ups' table there was constant conversation and laughter over the events of the week. Many bosses would have been surprised to hear the tales told about them at Sunday church dinner. In fact, some of them became so familiar to us they were asked about every week. "Say, Brother Brown, what was Steele up to this week?"

"That man is crazy. Do you know he thinks I believe he tried to get me a raise from the Big Boss?"

"What'd he say?"

"Come tellin' me he tried his best to convince the Big Boss that I was worth more than they was payin' me."

"Don't think he did that?" (Laughter.)

"Man, the Big Boss was out of town all last week. Not only is Steele crazy, but he thinks I'm crazy."

One of the reasons we children could be so quiet at our table was because the conversation was so interesting at the grown-ups' table.

From time to time the women's contest to see who could make the hottest chow-chow, a relish made with vegetables, was followed by the men's contest to see who could eat the most of the hottest.

But the main thing that stands out in my memory about Sunday church dinner was the blessing of the food.

"God, we thank you for your generous gifts of food, given on our behalf. We thank you for the talents you have given these women who prepared it. We thank you for our health so that we may enjoy your blessing. We thank you for each other. And while we are acknowledging our blessing do not think that we have forgotten those less fortunate than us. So, Heavenly Father, watch over and bless and heal those of our

GRADUATION DAY

Students from Seward Montessori celebrate graduation day on Lake Street in Minneapolis. After completing his Frogtown project, photographer Wing Young Huie turned his camera to documenting life on Lake Street for a Walker Art Center exhibit, three outdoor street shows, and a published portfolio with highlights from his five-hundred-plus images. (Photograph © Wing Young Huie)

number who can't be with us today. Seek out and find those of our families who are lost to us today and unite them once again. And God, we know you haven't forgotten the sinners; bring them in out of the cold. We know you haven't forgotten the sick; heal them. We know you haven't forgotten the tired; give them rest."

"Amen."

"Hallelujah."

"Praise His Name."

"And God, take care of our children here in our midst. Keep their hearts clean and pure and their bodies strong so that they will be able to serve you with vigor and vitality. We ask these things in the name of Jesus. Amen."

The length and fervor of the prayer depended on who was giving it. Sometimes the prayers were so long all the food was cold by the time we ate it, but no one seemed to notice except the children.

After dinner the tables and chairs were put back and the dishes were washed. The adults were quieter. Then there was a short time when the children were free to play before YPWW started.

The very young children (the people in our church always used the formal term for kids) were tucked away in little mother-made nests in the back rows of the church. When I was old enough to read, which was the criterion for YPWW membership, I would often yearn for the wonderful Sunday evenings in my little nest.

Sunday school was a good deal like kindergarten, except that everything revolved around the Bible. YPWW was a training ground for future leaders of the church and the community. The youngsters in YPWW produced Sunday youth services, which were held a few times each year. Just as the Young Soloist was found in the Sunday school choir, young men who had talent for preaching came forward in the

YPWW youth services. The study of the Bible was much more than learning verses and coloring pictures of baby Moses hidden in the rushes, as was done in Sunday school. YPWW taught religious concepts and church law. Most of the Sunday school teachers were YPWW graduates. Young people remained in YPWW until they were adults.

Immediately after YPWW, evening church service started. Actually, it didn't start, it just came to be. A few people were on their knees, silently praying, others were reading the Bible, some were talking quietly in serious tones of voice, and the rest seemed to be doing nothing, but their faces showed that their thoughts were active.

After I learned to read, I used this time to look through Mama's Bible. I realize now that it was bound in leather. Its thickness was doubled by all of the pieces of paper in it. Mama wrote down parts of the sermon and Bible verses and words to songs and sometimes people's addresses and recipes on little pieces of paper and she kept them in her Bible.

The pages were thin and made a soft ruffling sound when she turned them. I loved to look at the colored pictures of Moses and Abraham, the birth and crucifixion of Jesus, and the beautiful Garden of Gethsemane.

The Bible was never far from Mama's hand, but on Sunday evenings I got to hold it in my lap and look through all of the pieces of paper. And when Reverend Lawrence called out the text on which he was going to base his sermon, I looked up the verse for Mama.

One by one the members of the choir took their places on the chairs set up around the altar, instead of marching in as they did for morning service. As Reverend Lawrence approached the pulpit he softly started to sing a song. Something slow, half-remembered and, therefore, half-hummed. The pianist filled in a chord here and there. Members of the congregation began to focus their attention, still relaxed, nodding their heads from time to time, with some of them looking casually in the hymn book for the song.

Near the end of the song the preacher started turning the pages of his Bible, looking for his text. The song ended, the accompanist played softly.

The preacher would continue to turn pages.

"Help him, Jesus."

"Help him, Jesus."

"Help him."

"And God said unto Moses, 'Free my people.' And God said unto Moses, '*Free* my people.' And God said unto Moses, 'Free *my* people.' And *God* said unto Moses, 'Free my people.'"

The preacher read from his text and then preached on what he had read. He read from the next section of his text and preached from what he had read, again.

Slowly, but with purpose, he built the tension. He built it like a spiral in the air; each time a little higher, and between, relaxing a little, but not as much as before. And the congregation reflected the mood. They commented on his words, their voices growing louder, and someone got the "spirit" and had to be held down and fanned.

Sister Nelson started to speak in tongues and was joined by several of the other Sisters. Sister Jenkins started to cry at about the time the piano started to play; no song in particular, chords and runs. The preacher started a deep hum in between calls of "Praise His Name," "Thank you Jesus," and "My God is real."

The tempo and fullness of the piano picked up and a tambourine joined in. Feet picked up the beat as people started singing the song. It was always a fast song and sometimes the chorus was sung over and over again with everybody dancing in the aisles. And about the time everyone was sweating and breathing hard, the piano player slowed the beat down and people went back to their seats while the preacher wiped his face with a big white handkerchief and smiled and shook his head in pleasure.

"He's waiting for you. Tonight Jesus is waiting for you. He's waiting for you to come on home."

Reverend Lawrence seemed to be looking right at each person.

The pianist had drifted into "Softly and Tenderly" and Reverend Lawrence used the words of the song for the Invitational. "Softly and tenderly, Jesus is calling. If you've already given your life to God, then come on up to thank Him."

Before you knew it almost everyone was walking up the aisle. The new members were prayed over and the old members gave support to them.

After they all came back to their seats, tired but satisfied, the collection plate was passed. The preacher talked about something then, too, but no one listened. Everybody was busy getting money out, finding the children's clothes, arranging rides home, and looking after other details. Naturally, the offering was blessed, but this was a short prayer because by now people were all but walking out of the door.

No matter who gave us a ride home, the car was always so crowded I sat on Mama's lap. This was due not only to the shortage of cars, but to the fact that most of the members of Mama's church were pretty close to Mama's size.

I went to sleep every Sunday during the ride home, a sleep that was only partly interrupted by the trip into the house and the change into my bed clothes. I would remain in this half-sleep state until I felt Mama come to bed, then I moved over to her side of the bed until I was a part of her, and I slept.

CHAPTER FOUR

HISTORY, HOME, AND A LAND OF GHOSTS

"At the meeting of the rivers were two worlds. . ."
—Maud Hart Lovelace, *Early Candlelight*, 1929

Much history lies on this land. There are stories of battle, of salvation, and of simply surviving from day to day. The stories and essays collected in this chapter speak of the burdens of history—and of remembering the past.

LEFT: "**WITCH TREE VARIATION**"
Anishinaabe artist George Morrison's 1982 study of the sacred Witch Tree was made with pencil and pen and ink. (Minnesota Historical Society)

OPPOSITE PAGE: **WITCH TREE**
A full moon rises above Lake Superior and the sacred Witch Tree. Known to the Anishinaabe as Manido Geezhi-gans, *or Spirit Little Cedar Tree, this gnarled cedar is believed to have witnessed some four hundred winters. It has received offerings of tobacco from Native American hunters in birchbark canoes, stood as a landmark to passing voyageurs during the heyday of the fur trade, and was still clinging to its perch on Hat Point near Grand Portage as the iron ore boats plied Lake Superior. It continues to weather the great lake's storms today. (Photograph © Gary Alan Nelson)*

Giiwosebig: The Hunting Party

By Winona LaDuke

Native American activist Winona LaDuke's ceremonial name in the Ojibwe language translates as "Thunderbird Woman," a fitting name given its bearer's boundless energy, interests, and concerns.

Half Anishinaabe (Ojibwe/Chippewa) and half Jewish, LaDuke was raised in California, Oregon, and on the White Earth Reservation in northern Minnesota that she now calls home. Harvard-educated, she has devoted herself to fighting for human rights around the globe, from her founding of the White Earth Recovery Project that seeks to buy back reservation land for Native Americans to her journalistic endeavors that have appeared in magazines worldwide.

Published by Voyageur Press in 1997, LaDuke's first novel, *Last Standing Woman*, is a sprawling, epic story of seven generations of Anishinaabe at White Earth. The stories are told in a narrative style that represents a Native view of the circular nature of time. Blending legend and history, it is a monumental tale that stretches from the U.S.–Dakota Conflict of 1862 to the future, presenting a hopeful vision out of a troubled past.

This chapter from *Last Standing Woman* chronicling a modern-day "buffalo" hunting expedition ties together aspects of the history of U.S.–Anishinaabe relations, reservation life, and retribution in the form of "back rent."

"SHAMAN"

Anishinaabe artist Frank Big Bear's so-called "Warrior Series" presents a startling contrast of ancient images viewed through a modern eye. His shaman was drawn with prisma colored pencils on paper in 1993. (Bockley Gallery)

WHEN D-DAY LAUGHED, he sounded as though he was on the verge of death as he brought forth the wrath of thirty years of smoking, chewing tobacco, and alcohol. Inevitably, his heartiest of laughs ended with a long coughing and sputtering spell. The point was to laugh anyway.

D-Day was a short, sturdy man who watched the world from behind thick glasses set in ancient horn-rims. He carried in front of him a belly that had settled like a gunny sack of potatoes. His white, crew-cut hair glistened against his dark skin, his weathered hands whispered of years in the woods peeling pulp for logging companies, and his tongue spoke mostly Ojibwe. He preferred the nuance of his own language, and over time, age and amnesia had taken most of the English he knew and returned it to its source, a shelf of yellowing books in a boarding-school library somewhere faraway.

D-Day had been on the beaches of Normandy on June 6, 1944, one of the few Indians on the front lines of the invasion. The victory had stayed with him through time, as had the name and an incredibly shiny uniform, which he extracted from a cocoon of plastic for ceremonies, powwows, village events, and Veteran's Day each year.

Although Veteran's Day was over and done with for this year, the celebrations were still going strong. D-Day, Mesabe, and John Brown were silly, although not *waa-waa-*

shkeshi. The old men sat on the porch of the elders housing unit in White Earth village. They were all upstanding veterans of various wars, foreign and domestic. D-Day had his victory to brag about. Mesabe was a World War I vet, but he had returned without all the decorations that D-Day carried pinned on his uniform's chest. Now ninety-seven years of age, Mesabe had simply the honor of having lived. John Brown served a short stint in the Korean War and returned home to the safety of the reservation and his family. Each year for Veteran's Day, they gathered again, celebrating their wars and their own longevity.

Tonight they had been talking about a long time back, before any of them were born, but well within the stories of their parents and grandparents. It was Mesabe who was speaking: "I'm telling you, store-bought buffalo meat tastes different. It's not right, not the same."

D-Day and John Brown nodded their heads in time to his words.

"Long ago, buffalo roamed over the flat, western part of the reservation—before it was a reservation, remember. And in the late summer each year, the herd grazed the grasses of the Red River region. That was a good time. And that was good meat. Real live meat. Not like now."

"Not like now," D-Day echoed.

The old men were silent for a moment, all remembering the succulent taste of meat roasted over a fire.

"That was meat with spirit," said John Brown, licking his lips without thinking.

Mesabe continued: "The hunting parties were honored and important. The men were gone for days, traveling by horseback to find the buffalo herds. Then, after a successful hunt, two to three buffalo were cleaned, butchered, and brought home by horse and canoe. That was how we used to go. Remember, *ina*?"

"Now all the meat comes from the feedlot and is wrapped in paper," D-Day said, shaking his head, "paper with a stamp on it at Country Market. That's how Indians got to eat now."

ANISHINAABE COURTING FLUTE

This courting flute was carved by Minnesota Anishinaabe artist Jeffrey Chapman bearing the likeness of a loon's head, symbolic of the loonlike sounds the flute could make in the hands of a skilled musician or love-stricken suitor. Courting flutes were carved by the men of many Native American tribes to charm their beloved with music. As folklorist Frances Densmore wrote of the Anishinaabe flute-players in her Chippewa Customs *of 1929, "The flute was played by the men to attract and please young maidens." Speaking of the flute's legendary creation in* American Indian Myths and Legends, *Henry Crow Dog of the Brule Sioux told Richard Erdoes, "That flute of ours, the siyotanka, is for only one kind of music—love music."* (Courtesy of the Science Museum of Minnesota)

"NETT LAKE AUTUMN"
Anishinaabe artist Carl Gawboy's watercolor painting captures the mood of a fall day on the Nett Lake Reservation. (Minnesota Historical Society)

Summer had slowly eased into fall. Warm days lingered as long as they could until a crisp damp wind and a mist of rain fell on the land as always. Then a last dance of summer, one week of southern winds, sun, and a soft rain returned for that last, sweetest of memories.

It was late in the evening when Willie Schneider drove by with Alanis Nordstrom in his extended-cab pickup. The old men were still on the porch, still deliberating over the taste of buffalo and the virtues of different morsels. Mesabe waved them down. When Willie stopped, D-Day commandeered the pickup with Willie and Alanis as their chauffeurs. "*Equay, Ambe maajaa weesnik biziki.* Will you drive us?" D-Day asked as he pulled open the truck door. Before the surprised Willie could nod his head, the old men stumbled into the back seat, and the odor of aftershave, chew, and cigarettes filled the pickup. Alanis noticed that D-Day was carrying a rifle half hidden under his coat and Mesabe had a set of wire cutters held behind his back. John Brown's pocket bulged with the weight of a flashlight.

"What are you doing back in these parts?" Mesabe queried Alanis.

"I am just back to visit," she responded. "I had some vacation time due me and wanted to come see you all."

At that, the old men in the back of the truck giggled. Willie looked straight ahead, shyly watching the road.

"So, where are we going, *Mishom*?" Alanis asked, looking in the rearview mirror at their set faces.

"Lets head out by Mahnomen; there's plenty there," D-Day directed to the designated taxi service.

"Plenty of what?" Willie questioned him.

But the old men were silent, as if they had not heard him. They were all looking intently out the front window of the pickup.

"So where have you been tonight?" Mesabe finally said, as crafty as a fox.

Willie and Alanis professed that they had come from a late meeting at the land office when they had been flagged down. The tribal land program, with the hefty donation from Claire St. Clair, had managed to purchase a number of farms. Indian families from the HUD housing project in Minneapolis and the reservation were now moving into the farms. Willie served on the land committee, and Alanis showed up to watch the proceedings. Willie had been happy to see her there and offered her a ride home.

"This land's all ours, you know, Alanis," Mesabe pro-

nounced from the backseat, reaffirming Indian law as he did each day.

"Sure is," said Alanis. It was land these old men had known forever, but land until recently not owned on paper by Indians.

"No, I mean this land's really ours. Never mind the paper," Mesabe said. Alanis looked into the rearview mirror as Willie drove and saw Mesabe's eyes meet hers, glowing with ferocity even in the dark of night.

"No, I mean this land's really ours. Never mind the paper," Mesabe said. Alanis looked into the rearview mirror as Willie drove and saw Mesabe's eyes meet hers, glowing with ferocity even in the dark of night.

With the changes in land ownership wrought by the land programs, there was a change in natural resource management as well. Previously, the county commissioners had issued almost endless timber permits to companies from off the reservation with little of the money coming back to the Indians. Now, a natural resource management committee established a program of selective cutting and habitat restoration. The committee had planted medicinal plants and re-introduced animals. It also strictly limited hunting. Ten years prior, the majority of the deer and fish on the reservation had been taken by non-Indian sports hunters; today, the statistics were sharply reversed and the harvest was lower. Non-Indians could still hunt on the reservation, but they required a special permit.

Willie Schneider and Moose Hanford sparked the idea to issue the hunting permits based on income. "Sport hunting is a crime against the natural order and against the Anishinaabeg code of ethics," Hanford had said. "However, people who really need food have a right to take animals. We can figure out who those people are, in part, by income." Selam Big Bear had made the arguments for culture and residency as well. Big Bear sat on the Anishinaabeg citizenship committee.

Under new tribal enrollment provisions, a commitment to language and culture were now a central part of tribal membership. "It's not that you have to be a fluent Ojibwe speaker," Selam reasoned, "only that you should be sincere about a commitment to remembering your culture and language." Big Bear always used the term "remembering" when referring to language and culture since within the past four generations most people had spoken, but lost, the language. "Hey, it's not my fault, I can't speak Ojibwe," Big Bear would say. "Boarding schools and the Mahnomen principal made sure I couldn't even talk to my grandparents by the time they were through with me."

Willie Schneider turned the pickup down a dirt road following D-Day's insistent pointing finger.

Willie spoke up now. "So you guys going to do some hunting tonight, eh?"

He saw the way D-Day stirred uncomfortably in the seat with the .30–06 under his jacket.

"*Eh heh,*" came the response from the backseat.

Willie quietly slipped his arm around Alanis's shoulders, his movement a part of his conversation.

Mesabe smiled, observing the earnest doings of his young counterpart and empathizing with his challenge. Alanis was a headstrong and cosmopolitan woman who found herself struggling with all of her own expectations, standards, and what she loved. Willie Schneider reminded her of her father, the smell of his sweat, his big hands, and the security of his presence. Except Willie was not a ladies man, but the exact opposite. He was shy and unsure around women. But he was determined. He had set his sight on Alanis and somehow was going to win her heart. The old way, maybe.

"Ever hear an Ojibwe flute?" Mesabe asked Alanis from the back seat of the big truck. Mesabe had read Willie's mind, and he could see Willie shift in his seat.

"No, can't say I have."

"Those Ojibwe love songs on a flute are really something."

"No kidding?" Alanis's voice raised slightly to show her interest and hide her amusement. She shifted slightly, aware of Willie's arm at her back. "Been giving any lessons lately, *Mishom*?"

She smiled into the rearview mirror at the old man who chuckled now. Mesabe elbowed D-Day and whispered something to him in Ojibwe and they all laughed. D-Day's was his loud, raspy laugh. Alanis looked again at the old man and smiled at Willie. She was not sure how she felt about him, but his arm around her shoulder was okay for now. Maybe she would wait for the flute.

"Slow down!" shouted John Brown, and a startled Willie lifted his foot off the gas.

"Turn off them headlights," Mesabe interjected.

The headlights went out, and the world around them turned dark.

"What's going on?" Alanis asked. But Willie suddenly knew where they were and why they were there.

They were driving slowly now onto the outlying land of a large cattle ranch owned by a woman from Oklahoma. The five-thousand-acre spread adjoined tribal land in a couple of places, and had been the center of controversy over the

"What are you guys doing?" Alanis whispered. "I'm collecting back rent," D-Day said out loud, and his two buddies almost fell over themselves laughing.

past few years. The Oklahoma woman had never even seen this ranch, named Oxblood. She had inherited it from her grandfather, a big land speculator who had picked up sixty or so allotments decades past. Now she ran the ranch as a corporation from her headquarters a thousand miles away. Over the past two years there had been a number of skirmishes between the ranch operators and the tribe, mostly over environmental problems. A feed lot in the northeast corner drained directly into the Wild Rice River, and sewage and pesticides were ending up downstream. Although the environmental department had issued a series of warnings and tried to condemn the site more than once, the operators would invariably hire an attorney, find a loophole, and restart.

Then there was the problem of the native prairie grasses. The Oxblood Ranch was home to a number of patches of the native prairie grasses the tribe wanted to protect. Although the Indians had tried to purchase conservation easements, the owners were adamant that no Indian had any business on the ranch. A number of the areas had highly prized medicinal plants that tribal members often harvested, now mostly in secret to avoid the No Trespassing signs. People always reported fewer plants to harvest in each subsequent year, but the tribe seemed powerless to stop the destruction. After two years, negotiations had broken down, as had the patience of many tribal members.

Aside from these troubles, everyone knew that D-Day's family had owned four of the allotments that now comprised the Oxblood Ranch.

It was a moonless night with a warm southerly wind. Willie eased the pickup down a section road adjoining the ranch. The old men lost their silliness and commenced thinking about the importance of their mission. About a mile and a half down the road, Willie halted the pickup in response to John Brown's whispered command.

"Where are we?" Alanis whispered, but her question was not answered.

D-Day was the first out, followed by the other three. The old man took tobacco from his pouch and passed some to Willie, who grinned as he accepted it, realizing he was now an accomplice. He was a Vietnam vet, so maybe he was being made an honorary member of the hunting party.

John Brown broke the head off a Marlboro cigarette and passed a second to Mesabe. Each man said a few words and set tobacco out under a large white pine near the truck. Only then did they extract the rifle, wire cutters, and flashlights from the truck. Then Mesabe went back and laboriously lifted himself into the driver's seat.

Prepared, D-Day and John Brown headed off through the woods toward the ranchland. In his usual good spirits, Mesabe began to giggle from the rear guard. He watched the two old men shuffle through the woods toward the fence. Having arrived at his predetermined site, D-Day extracted his wire cutters.

"What are you guys doing?" Alanis whispered, looking with wide eyes from D-Day's wire cutters to the faraway lights of the ranchhouse. "What's going on?"

"I'm collecting back rent," D-Day said out loud, and his two buddies almost fell over themselves laughing.

D-Day neatly cut through the four barbed-wire strands as John Brown pulled them back. Just for good measure, D-Day repeated this exercise every two hundred and fifty feet or so along the fence.

This pasture held the Simmentals. These were special cows that tasted real good. The White Faces were in the feeding lot, but they were less interesting. "After all," D-Day had reasoned back at the elder's home, "you could buy them at the Country Market store along with that funny buffalo meat." The Simmentals also like to roam, and at fifteen hundred dollars apiece, that roaming was a good investment of their time.

After they finished up the east pasture, the two old men trundled over to the workhorses. The owners of the Oxblood bred Percherons, the kind of horse D-Day and Mesabe had used in their days on the logging crews. Those horses knew how to move as well, and with a couple of big gaps in their fences, chances were those horses could be almost in Mahnomen by morning. Watching the two old men from the truck, Mesabe spoke to Willie in a whisper: "The horses aren't for eating. It's just the principle of the thing."

Willie shook his head, thinking to himself, "Besides, horse stealing was an old Indian trick, and these are old Indians."

Alanis whispered into Mesabe's ear, "What are you doing now? What if someone sees us?"

Mesabe only giggled again and said, "You watch for lights from the ranchhouse over there." And he pointed a gnarled finger to the west.

Now the hunting could begin. D-Day positioned himself on the side of the fence that was tribal land and waited, cradling the heavy rifle in his unsteady hands. John Brown moved in toward the herd. He set his sights on a cow, fat, but not too old, or too heavy. And she should be tender. Waving his arms in the air, he drove most of the animals toward the fence, keeping a close eye on the heifer. A flashlight illumi-

nated their escape route.

As the animals saw the hole, they accelerated. A surge of fifty cows rushed through the fence. The heifer stayed toward one side and in easy range of D-Day. As the animals set hoof on tribal land, Mesabe hit the headlights of the pickup. The lights stunned the animals and they stood stock still. John Brown motioned to D-Day to take a shot.

The shot almost put the old man on his ass. The cow fell at once, and the other three men cried out in a high-pitched "counting coup" call.

"*Howah!*" D-Day exclaimed. He was exhilarated. "I shot a buffalo."

The rest of the frightened herd scattered into the woods except a few of the less intelligent beasts, who stared with vacant eyes at the fallen cow and the old men. D-Day took out his tobacco pouch again as he slowly walked toward the cow. Her face still hot, he put some tobacco in her mouth and kneeled down by her side. He put his hand on the side of her head and spoke softly to her and thanked her for her life: "*Mashkode biizhiki, mashkode biizhiki.*"

Alanis looked nervously around to make sure no one at the ranchhouse could see them. The house and the watchdogs were a thousand acres away, so there was little danger. Willie perched himself on the pickup's roof just to make sure: The old men may have been slow, but they were accomplished hunters at this stage in their lives. *Awakaanag.* Accomplished hunters—especially of domesticated animals.

With jerks and starts, Mesabe backed the truck up to tow the cow. In different circumstances, they would have gutted the animal there but the Oxblood Ranch security might have heard the shots. Willie jumped out with a come-along in his hand. He hooked the come-along on the back side of the truck cab and quickly unwound it toward the cow. The old men maneuvered a blanket under the cow, end by end, as the strap of the come-along was fit snugly around both the blanket and the cow. The old men guided the cow, and Willie cranked the come-along. As the cow inched up toward the truck, John Brown and Willie changed places. With a grunt, the younger man shoved the cow into the truck.

Willie buttoned up the back of the truck, and everyone climbed back into the cab. John Brown was shouting "*Howah!*" in imitation of D-Day, and Mesabe was giggling. Even Willie and Alanis were feeling silly now as D-Day laughed and coughed and rubbed a shoulder sore from the kick of the rifle. The truck slowly moved down the section road and out onto Highway 200. Only then did Willie turn on the headlights.

ABANDONED FARMSTEAD
A forsaken farmhouse and outbuilding wait out their days in Lincoln County. (Photograph © Gary Alan Nelson)

The Visible Dead

By Bill Holm

William Jon Holm is a poet laureate of small towns everywhere. He is part prairie radical, part village agnostic, and part town crier. His writings may remind readers of Sinclair Lewis and Walt Whitman, but ultimately he has a voice that is all his own.

Holm calls home the small Minnesota prairie town of Minneota, where he was born in 1943. Along with teaching at Southwest State University in Marshall, he has taught American literature at the University of Iceland in Reykjavik and at China's Xi'an Jiaotong University. He is the author of several books of poems, including *The Dead Get By With Everything* and *Boxelder Bug Variations*, as well as a number of books of essays and prose, such as *The Music of Failure*, *Coming Home Crazy: An Alphabet of China Essays*, and *The Heart Can Be Filled Anywhere on Earth: Minneota, Minnesota*.

This elegy to Minnesota's graveyards comes from Holm's book of essays, *Landscape of Ghosts*, published by Voyageur Press. As he wrote half in jest in the book's introduction, it is a volume "full of pictures of stuff nobody wants to look at and of essays on subjects no one wants to read about." To Holm, a cemetery is much more. It is a remembrance of things past, a history carved in granite that will endure.

THE VISIBLE DEAD
A lone tombstone in a prairie graveyard glows in the last light of evening. (Photograph © Bob Firth/Firth Photo Bank)

AMERICA COULD HARDLY have done better for a common language than English. All the myths we believe about ourselves as a country and a culture, while they may be only a quarter- or half-true, otherwise are completely accurate as descriptions of our language habits. English was born of a miscegenated marriage of elegant French and blunt Saxon; it has no morals or standards; it takes any bastard word from anywhere into its house and lets it breed; it opens its arms to the poor, the tired, and the homeless with far more joy and ease than the country itself ever mustered. We are a kind of Ellis Island of language; words came through our doors and, with greater speed and efficiency than most inhabitants, melted down quickly into common speech. As a result, our word horde is vast and many-leveled—maybe the vastest of any language in history. Since we are spiritual Texans to a fault and love to boast of size and magnitude, American English presents us with an opportunity to tell the truth for a change.

But one gift from our outsized polyglot language is the power to shade and dissipate meaning almost into vapor. Geniuses at euphemism, we find softer, vaguer, more disconnected words for facts that seem unpleasant to us. We pass away, go to rest, or are interred in Sunset Memorial Gardens or some such place, where the lawn is meticulous and stones don't show bad manners by visibly standing up to be counted. Perhaps not by coincidence, two of our distinguished literary reminders of the hard facts of death, both linguistic and otherwise, Jessica Mitford and Evelyn Waugh, were British, the custodians of our language before Americans opened their doors wide to the world's linguistic riff-raff. If we want to take a little of the sting out of death and make the grave think twice about victory, we will damn well do it! It's a free country! Why else would we have thrown all that tea into Boston Harbor?

The euphemisms of death, however, are city luxuries of a habited place with money, distractions, and other matters on its mind. On the plains, in immigrant places, the visible graves stand up not in memorial gardens, but in graveyards. They exist in plain Saxon, not having cultivated French manners to soften and civilize them. A yard of graves. That's what they are . . . a field of bones, stones, and language that contains some information maybe useful to us, if we are alert to it.

In the Minneota countryside, you can do a rudimentary ethnic census, a social and economic history, a survey of aesthetic taste and religious preference, all on a Sunday afternoon saunter down township roads. Investigate the graveyards and question the stones. You will find the inhabitants cooperative—up to a point.

There are three kinds of rural graveyards. The first kind huddle around their country church like a field of petrified corn. Sometimes, since rural churches have gone mostly the way of rural schools and given up the ghost themselves, the church will have disappeared from its foundations, leaving only the graveyard. Do these churches evaporate as the parish ages and the town church beckons? Some burn on windy nights, leaving only naked foundations; some have their lumber recycled by thrifty farmers into barns and houses; some are sold, then picked up and moved to new spots to become churches for younger more enthusiastic denominations; some simply collapse into handsome ruins, and are left for the graveyard maintenance committee to clean up.

The Icelandic Lutheran church in Westerheim township, where most of my relatives are buried and where I am a small landowner myself, closed its doors in the early fifties after the neighborhood Icelandic farmers had moved to town, sent their children off to college and away from the farm, or failed to breed a new generation of steady, firmly rooted Lutherans. The Church Board, finding the old church sound of limb, sold it to the Baptists, who had more fervor and more use for a previously owned church. I can't remember whether I was there at the moving or not, but the story is so locally notorious that I made myself a retroactive spectator. The movers successfully moved the church off its foundations and onto a flatbed for its trip down the county road. All was ready, the power lines disconnected in the right places, and the sheriff's lights flashing to head the slow procession. The flatbed inched forward with caution and majesty; after a few feet, the sturdy-looking Icelandic church collapsed in on itself with dramatic finality with great clouds of dust. Poor luck for the Baptists . . . "Just like a damned Icelander!" muttered one old farmer. "Too proud and bull-headed to move . . ." But the neatly tended graveyard remained on its corner. The stones faced west to supervise the ghost of the dead church that once kept them company.

Sometimes a country church seems never to have wanted its graveyard close at hand, and banished it to the next section on some bare and windy spot. Driving down the road, you are startled to see a wrought-iron fence and a nicely mowed graveyard with a couple of trees to shade the dead, surrounded by a thrashing ocean of alfalfa or wheat. Maybe, the old settlers thought, the dead needed a little privacy, too and wanted a special trip to visit them. Or maybe the land was cheap.

Finally, there are graveyards themselves, "a fine and private place," sometimes only a grave or two in an open field or next to what was once a farmstead. Why here, alone, rather than in a community of the dead? Perhaps the farmers wanted to plant something more permanent of themselves next to their own crops on their own land. This was, after all, for a

GRAVEYARD
A crescent moon shines over a country graveyard. (Photograph © Bob Firth/Firth Photo Bank)

GHOSTS
Like bizarre agricultural sculptures, obsolete threshing machines from days gone by sit out the years perched on prairie hilltops in Kandiyohi County. (Photograph © Gary Alan Nelson)

great majority of Minnesota immigrants, their first chance in history to be landowners rather than hired hands, even semifeudal serfs who brought up the rear guard of the European class system. If we bury grandpa and the baby lost in childbirth in our own yard, it will give us a tentacle into history; enough graves and the north eighty will become an ancestral estate. Or perhaps there were immigrants so wounded and disillusioned by institutions like state and church that they wanted no truck with them in death, the last great unbureaucratic privacy.

Will Weaver, the northern Minnesota writer, has a wonderful short story called "A Gravestone Made of Wheat," where he posits both of these possibilities. A proud old Nor-

wegian, told by the sheriff that it is now illegal for environmental reasons to bury his wife Inge in his own farmyard, thinks back on a half century of pettiness and abuse from local power, then plows the old lady into the middle of a wheat field by moonlight. She's safe from the sheriff, and her sons will always be able to find her where the wheat is a few inches taller than its unfertilized neighbors.

No township in Minnesota is without these private lonesome graves. They are local touchstones, scenic attractions, and breeding grounds for folklore. Ask at the coffee shop downtown; you'll find out where they are and hear stories. Between Sleepy Eye and New Ulm, a folklorist friend of mine found a grave of a six-year-old girl dead in the 1880s, lying in the middle of a field between two trees, the place reputedly haunted. He had heard local yarns of visitations, spectres, odd lights, moaning that was not the wind, damp white dresses, and grass that refused to grow. A bunch of us decided to investigate: the folklorist, a couple of writers, a photographer with infrared filters, and a skeptic. We went at sundown and stayed until dark. We drank wine and told stories. The photographer got fine and eerily colored pictures, probably because the earth itself is a fine and eerie place, but the skeptic seemed to have won the night. Nothing supernatural happened except a bunch of friends having a good time at a lovely and lonesome spot. Who's to say that's not enough?

Around my hometown, I send visitors to two grave sites. A single white marble military gravestone with an Irish name and the number of a Civil War regiment stands in a field along the highway a mile from the almost entirely Belgian village of Ghent. Did the Irishman not want to lie down with Belgians? Was he the only Protestant in a Catholic town? The only veteran among pacifists? There are probably answers to these questions, but I am not interested nor, I feel sure, is McQuestion, the dead veteran in his private national cemetery. He is visually handsome in white marble surrounded sometimes by clover, alfalfa, thistles, prairie grass, and sometimes by ice and snowdrifts that almost cover him up. He says "Kilroy was here . . ." by whatever name.

One of my great-granduncles, a homesteader north of Minneota, was a local grandee. He had somehow made money in Iceland, traveled to Denmark, and become worldly before arriving north of Minneota. He indentured his brothers' passages to America (as I have heard the story) and did little work himself. He read, and sent the only two of his many children of two marriages who survived past thirty to the university. The brother and sister came home after his death, tended his farms, read more books, threw nothing away for fifty years, and never went to church. Among their books were Voltaire, Thomas Paine, and Robert Ingersoll, signs of free thinking, and Madame Blavatsky and Anne Besant, signs of theosophical inclinations. Neither of the children ever married, and when they died, in the 1960s, they went back of the grove to join father, mother, and a handful of stepbrothers and stepsisters, all dead either in infancy or early youth. The house, with most of the accumulated packrattery, burned the night after the sale, and the new landowners tore down the now collapsing round barn that once made the farm a landmark. Nothing left but the family graveyard with its almost haughty aristocratic privacy and its nice sense of completeness and finality—all the relatives safely home at last.

It's a wonderful place, behind its fence, next to a muddy river, a little island of the dead surrounded now by a sea of corn and beans, so arrogantly growing, so happily alive. It comforts me a little to see this visible language of graves, to live as its neighbor. A culture that hides its verbal facts will not care very intelligently for its physical facts either. We must both look at things clearly and name them right.

If you want to know something of the history of settlement in a Minnesota township, ask the dead. The living are busy with work, church, or television, and have begun making up new answers, or to put it in an American way: to reinvent the past, to make it "all new in through here . . ."

But the language knocked into marble or granite will give you a few facts if you know how to read them. The road from Minneota through Lincoln County to the South Dakota border goes past graveyards of Icelanders, Norwegians, Germans, Danes, Poles, a scattering of Yankees and Irish, and a few

BOOT HILL
Boots adorn fence posts along a Kandiyohi County road. (Photograph © Gary Alan Nelson)

ONE-ROOM SCHOOLHOUSE
The days of the one-room country schoolhouse are all but gone except in the most isolated parts of the country. This empty schoolhouse sits on the prairie in Ottertail County, lonely for the sounds of children. (Photograph © Gary Alan Nelson)

failed Civil War veteran farmers. A few miles in the opposite direction will take you past Belgians, Dutch, and Swedes. If you ask these graveyards questions, here's a few of the things they might tell you. Who was broke in Europe and when? When did the land in the old country give out? How far had the railroad gotten built? Where hadn't the homestead land run out? Look at the stone piles and the soil quality in neighboring fields. Who got there first to claim the best and who arrived last to inherit the gullies? How many graves of women dead in childbirth or children in infancy? That's a fair gauge of poverty, trouble, and the misery of transplanting. How quickly did English get learned and assimilation start?

In the age of the bilingual education debate ad nauseam, a graveyard will give you a lesson in how assimilation happens. Here's a hypothetical example from an Icelandic graveyard: the history of how the spelling of a common name decomposes.

Memory is the language of graveyards.

GUÐMUNDSSON—The original and correct spelling with an odd letter not in the modern English alphabet: Ð with a slash pronounced *th*, and with correct grammar: the genitive double *s*. This name is a patronymic in the old country and is good only through one generation, and then only for sons. "Dottir" for daughters: Gudmundsdottir.

GUDMUNDSON—Now we have taken citizenship for which you need a permanent last name even for daughters who, after all, are not sons, by neither linguistic nor sexual logic. Here in the New World you can't go changing your name every generation to confuse the neighbors and the tax board—unless you are a gambler. Here we must be like our neighbors, even if nothing in our own language demands it. No double *s,* and a hard *d.*

GUDMANSON—Here the name has started to respect American phonetics, no consonantal blocks to slow you down on the road to prosperity and the middle class.

GOODMANSON—Now, it's begun to look like a real American word! Even the ghost of the aspirated *GUÐ,* (pronounced Gvuth), has died away to become "GOOD" in all senses. Ironically, straight hair used to be called "good hair" in the Black community for years. At least the pink Icelanders didn't have to buy straightening chemicals . . . just changed the spelling.

GOODMAN—Almost a politically correct name; half of the cumbersome gender distinction atrophied away like a leprous limb and fallen into the ash heap of our fast history. It now bears only a ghostly resemblance to its Icelandic ancestry and could safely be carved in any graveyard in New England without disturbing the old settlers. That name can go to Minneapolis and get a good job, carry credit cards, own personal computers, and jog!

It hasn't happened yet, or at least I haven't seen it, but that name will soon be GOOD. Something is gained in that process, but something is lost, too. We've got an American now, but without much memory.

This decomposition took hardly two generations, sixty or seventy years. In a city, it might have gone even faster. A few miles down the road from the Icelanders, the Poles had been at work adding vowels to names like CZK for a couple of generations. Soon the Slavs and the Vikings will look so much alike in granite that they won't remember the insults, invasions, and old quarrels over the last thousand or so years. As Europe in 1992 began erupting into its old ethnic savagery, Americans ought to be at least a little grateful for that process.

Memory is the language of graveyards. It is not so easy to carve words in hard stone to as spit them out of a laser printer or fax them on a memorandum. So language becomes dense and heavy—just a name, some dates, a snatch of a hymn, or an old saying. Euphemisms cost too much to chisel so we dispense with them. The old graveyards that populate the countryside in Minnesota—and everywhere—are good neighbors both spiritually and visibly. They are frequently lovely places, filled with fine shadows and angles and light, gifts for the painter or photographer. They contain the rudiments of our common history, reminding us of who we now are, who got us to that point, and what at least one part of our future looks like, if we are able to see it with a steely eye. Finally, on a fine July day, the air perfumed with the damp smell of mown grass, and loud with mourning doves and meadowlarks singing requiem (or whatever those noises mean), it's pleasant to think, as Walt Whitman did, of all this sweet earth being continually fed by all those sour dead. Just another miracle in a long string.

Home Is a Place in Time

By Paul Gruchow

Paul Gruchow's love for the Minnesota prairie stems from his youth, coming of age on his family's farm near Montevideo. That passion for "empty spaces," as he has called it, has never left him.

Gruchow worked for several decades as a journalist. He began in his high school days, writing an early column for the Montevideo *American-News*, graduated to edit the University of Minnesota's *Minnesota Daily*, before working for a time at Minnesota Public Radio. As managing editor and part owner of the Worthington *Daily Globe*, he built the newspaper into a unique rural paper with a strong voice, a journalistic town crier.

Through his books, Gruchow has celebrated the landscape of Minnesota. His first book was a collection of observances, *Journal of a Prairie Year*. It was followed by further essays on our sense of place, including *The Necessity of Empty Places* and *Grass Roots: The Universe of Home*, from which this essay is taken. In addition, Gruchow is the author of *Minnesota: Images of Home* with photographer Jim Brandenburg, *Travels in Canoe Country*, and *Boundary Waters: The Grace of the Wild*.

"THE CLOUD"
Many Minnesota farm youths found ample reasons to halt their chores for a rest while they explored the world around them. Artist Francis Lee Jaques painted this portrait of himself as a boy of twelve or thirteen contemplating the majesty of the clouds as his plow lay idle and his team of horses lunched on prairie grass. It was this fascination with nature that lead Jaques to become an artist, painting and drawing images of the natural world that graced museum dioramas at the James Ford Bell Museum of Natural History in Minneapolis, as well as magazines covers, bird guides, and his own books. (James Ford Bell Museum of Natural History)

WHAT IF ONE'S life were not a commodity, not something to be bartered to the highest bidder, or made to order? What if one's life were governed by needs more fundamental than acceptance or admiration? What if one were simply to stay home and plant some manner of garden?

To plant a garden is to enter the continuum of time. Each seed carries in its genome the history that will propel it into the future, and in planting it we stretch one of the long threads of our culture into tomorrow.

A home, like a garden, exists as much in time as in space. A home is the place in the present where one's past and one's future come together, the crossroads between history and heaven. I learned this truth the day we buried my mother.

In the previous month, I had felt often like a man without an anchor. We were living in St. Paul and expecting our first child. For my wife it was a difficult and somewhat dangerous pregnancy. Christmas passed and the days turned toward the new year. The baby was overdue. In those same days, Mother was lying in a hospital bed in Montevideo, Minnesota, emaciated and in pain. She had already lost a brave battle against cancer but was unwilling, just yet, to concede defeat, for reasons that were, to me, mysterious. She was long past delusion about her prospects. My own heart resided in both places, full of fear and hope at the same time. I did not know where my body should be.

On the penultimate day of the old year, the baby, after a stubborn resistance of her own, finally came. She was big and beautiful and healthy. She gave one lusty cry as she entered the world and then lay quietly while she was bathed and dressed, looking about the room in wide-eyed wonder.

I telephoned Mother with the news. She said with surprising energy that she hoped she might see the baby before she died. But that day a fierce cold front had settled over Minnesota. For more than a week daytime temperatures did not rise above zero. We were, as I suppose first-time parents always are, terrified of our responsibilities. The baby seemed so helpless and fragile. We did not dare risk the three-hour drive to the hospital.

One cloudy morning in mid-January the weather at last broke. We bundled up the baby and made a dash for Montevideo. In the darkened hospital room, we introduced grandmother and granddaughter. The baby slept against the rails of the bed while Mother fondled her with eyes too small for their bony sockets. They joined hands, the baby's soft, fat, and warm, Mother's cold, gaunt, and hard. With tremendous effort, Mother whispered three words barely audible above the hum of the humidifier.

"Is she healthy?" she asked. We wept, because she was.

When we arrived back home, the telephone was ringing. A nurse was on the line with the word, hardly news, that Mother had died.

The weather was still bitter and gray the day we buried her in the little cemetery at St. John's Lutheran Church. After the ceremony the three children—Kathy, Paulette, and I—who felt strangely like children again that day, vulnerable and bewildered in an impossibly big world, took refuge one last time in the farmhouse where we had laughed and cried, together and alone, so many times.

We had meant to see to the household goods. There would not be many other opportunities for it; we lived at a distance from one another and seldom found ourselves together. But almost the first items we came across were the photo albums. We sat in the living room then, not bothering to light the lamp, looking at the pictures and talking until the day died.

"Do you remember when Mother turned toward the back seat of the car and said, 'Where's your sister?' and Paul said, 'Oh, she fell out a long time ago,' and she *had*?"

"Do you remember the day Mother told the neighbor she couldn't go to the Women's Christian Temperance Union meeting because her wine was ready for bottling?"

"Do you remember the day Kathy fell through the outhouse hole?"

"'Do you remember the day you rode your bicycle down the driveway with no hands and it made me so mad I stomped the spokes out of my bicycle's wheels?"

"Do you remember the time we floated a pound of butter in Mother's hot laundry starch?"

Do you remember?

Do you remember?

The stories tumbled as if out of an overstuffed closet. Sometimes we had three of them going at once. We laughed until we ached. I remember it now as one of the happiest afternoons of my life, the metamorphosis of a friendship deepening as the years pass and we three face our own mortalities. I think that I have never been more exactly at home, more tenaciously alive, than that afternoon, when old joy and new sorrow and present love reverberated together inside me.

All history is ultimately local and personal. To tell what we remember, and to keep on telling it, is to keep the past alive in the present. Should we not do so, we could not know, in the deepest sense, how to inhabit a place. To inhabit a place means literally to have made it a habit, to have made it the custom and ordinary practice of our lives, to have learned

All history is ultimately local and personal.

152

HIKERS
The fall foliage beckons along the Arrowhead Trail. (Photograph © Layne Kennedy)

APPLE PICKERS
A crew of apple pickers rest their arms on the hood of their trusty Massey-Ferguson tractor during the annual apple harvest at Pepin Heights Orchard in Lake City. (Photograph © Layne Kennedy)

Memories
of a
Former Kid

By Bob Artley

For several decades, artist Bob Artley has collected his remin-iscences of the farming life into a syndicated cartoon series entitled "Memories of a Former Kid," which originated in the Worthington Daily Globe *newspaper. His drawings and essays have also been collected into several books, including* Memories of a Former Kid, Cartoons II, *and* A Book of Chores As Remembered by a Former Kid.

These drawings recall life on the family farm through the four seasons and the many adventures that befell country youths.

how to wear a place like a familiar garment, like the garments of sanctity that nuns once wore. The word habit, in its now-dim original form, meant to own. We own places not because we possess the deeds to them, but because they have entered the continuum of our lives. What is strange to us—unfamiliar—can never be home.

It is the fashion just now to disparage nostalgia.

Nostalgia, we believe, is a cheap emotion. But we forget what it means. In its Greek roots it means, literally, the return to home. It came into currency as a medical word in nineteenth-century Germany to describe the failure to thrive of the displaced persons, including my own ancestors, who had crowded into that country from the east. Nostalgia is the clinical term for homesickness, for the desire to be rooted in a place—to know clearly, that is, what time it is. This desire need not imply the impulse to turn back the clock, which of course we cannot do. It recognizes, rather, the truth—if home is a place in time—that we cannot know where we are now unless we can remember where we have come from. The real romantics are those who believe that history is the story of the triumphal march of progress, that change is indiscriminately for the better. Those who would demythologize the past seem to forget that we also construct the present as a myth, that there is nothing in the wide universe so vast as our own ignorance. Knowing that is our one real hope.

ABOVE AND RIGHT: **HOME SWEET ICE HOUSE**
Ice houses turn into winter homes-away-from-home on Lake Mille Lacs. (Photographs by Layne Kennedy)

WINTER LIGHTS
A pine tree decked in lights glows in the midst of a blue northwoods night. (Photograph © Richard Hamilton Smith)

Permissions